HASLAM
OVER THE YEARS

MARGARET LILY HARTSHORN

ASHRIDGE PRESS/COUNTRY BOOKS

Published by Ashridge Press/Country Books
Courtyard Cottage, Little Longstone, Bakewell, Derbyshire DE45 1NN

ISBN 1 901214 33 8

British Library Cataloguing in Publication Data.
A catalogue record for this book is available from the British Library.

ACKNOWLEDGEMENTS
Many thanks to the following people for helping to make this book possible:

Ann Krawszik, Local Studies Department, Chesterfield Library.
Mike Wilson, Editor of The Derbyshire Times, Chesterfield.
Mr Gilby, Hasland Junior School.
The many people who loaned the photographs which are included.
The people who related to me their memories of Hasland
and allowed me to include them in this book.

Title page:
A group of children near the Toll Bar, 1915.

Printed and bound by Antony Rowe Ltd.
Chippenham, Wiltshire

CONTENTS

The shops and Toll Bar, Hasland, 1910.
Photograph courtesy of Mary Boden.

The shops and Toll Bar, Hasland, 2002.

INTRODUCTION

I was born in Hasland and my parents were Jesse and Doris Shaw. My mother's family came to Hasland in the late 19th century for work in the collieries, and my father came to work at the Hasland Loco Shed around 1930.

After researching my family history for several years, this led to me taking a keen interest in the local history of Hasland where I have spent all my life. During the research into my family I have accumulated rather a lot of information on the village from censuses, directories and local newspapers, and I thought that perhaps it may be of interest to other local residents. I have also recorded the memories of several older people who grew up in the village, which I have included in this book. I would like to say that information regarding the past is sometimes very conflicting and people's memories differ, therefore I appreciate that this account may contain some inaccuracies. However, the main facts are sound and I hope that many people will enjoy this record of Hasland and it's people.

I would like to dedicate this book to my husband Graham, to Sharon, Mick, Kevin and Suzanne, and of course my grandchildren Craig, Ryan, Laura, Jordan and Adam.

Map of Hasland, 1918.

Elm Tree Farm, Hasland Road.
Photograph courtesy of Robert Wood

The orchard and paddock of Green House Farm, Hasland, c1935.
Photograph courtesy of Bill Ervine.

FARMS

Hasland is situated approximately 2 miles in a south-easterly direction from Chesterfield in Derbyshire. It was taken into the Chesterfield Borough boundary in 1910. Many people still refer to it as a village, but over the years it has expanded greatly. In it's early days however it was a very rural community consisting of a few older properties and several farms. The following are some of the farms which have existed in Hasland through the years.

Elm Tree Farm was situated at the westerly side of Eastwood Park on the main Hasland Road. In 1851 Francis Lowe, his wife Elizabeth and their three month old son Thomas were in residence at this farm. Over the years they had several more children and two of their daughters later became teachers at the Church School. Francis and Elizabeth remained at the farm until their respective deaths in 1902 and 1904. The property remained in the Lowe family for many years until in 1971 Dorothy Lowe sold the farm and a large amount of land to the Land Commission. The farm was eventually demolished, a new road was constructed, and many houses built on the site. This is now the Eastwood Park Estate.

Whitebank Farm was situated at the top of a drive which was opposite St. Leonard's Drive on Hasland Road. There is now an estate of houses on the site.

Hall Farm was actually in the grounds of Hasland Hall and was situated on the easterly side of Hasland Green close to what is now the first entrance to Hasland Hall School. It was in the stables there that the first Hasland School was established.

Green Farm on Hasland Green has been occupied by the Hollingworth family for many years. In 1841 Joseph Hollingworth who was born in Ashover was a farmer living in Hasland with his wife Hannah and their three children William, Jane and Charles. In 1851 Joseph and Hannah were still said to be living in Hasland village. Charles was the only child still at home, and as yet unmarried. Joseph and Charles were still farming and they had one servant and a lodger living with them at this time. Charles married Elizabeth Bower at St. Paul's Church, Hasland in 1852 and by 1871 they were living on Mansfield Road and Charles was farming 10 acres of land. At this time they had two of their children, William and Ann Elizabeth, living with them. By 1881 they had moved to Green Farm and Charles, now 56 years old, was still a farmer but he now had 36 acres of land. They had their daughter Elizabeth living with them and also their son William, his wife Hannah and their two grand-children.

William and Hannah had seven children, which, I would imagine, was a great help when they had a farm to run. They also had one servant to help them for most

Green Farm, Hasland, c1950.
Photograph courtesy of Evelyn Hollingworth.

of the time. William was appointed Surveyor of Highways to the Parish Council prior to the Local Government Act of 1894. He held the post for just over a year. He was also a sidesman at St. Paul's Church for many years, and he attended the Grammar School in Chesterfield. He built several houses in Hasland including the row of terraced houses named Kimberley Terrace on Hampton Street. He had two personal tragedies in his life after his wife died in 1909. His son William Henry was a victim of the influenza epidemic in 1913, and another son Charles Cuthbert was killed in the Great War.

The Hollingworth family were tenants of Green Farm until William purchased it in 1913 after the death of the landowner Bernard Lucas.

William died in 1928 and his son Frank took over the farm after his death. Frank had previously married Ethel Vincent of Grassmoor and their son Charles Vincent was born in 1925. The Hollingworth family continued to work the farm, as Charles (or Chuck as he was known) also ran the farm after his father's death, until his own retirement. He had his own milk round which was started previously by his father. In those days, you had your milk round allocated to you, and I am sure that many

Hasland residents can remember him delivering the milk to their doorstep.

The farmhouse is still standing today although it is now a private dwelling.

Greenhouse Farm was situated on Hasland Green and during the 20th century the Heathcote family resided there for many years. In 1951 there was a very bad fire in a Dutch barn when it was completely gutted and the entire contents destroyed. Apparently this was only one of several fires which occurred at this farm. Although the other farm buildings have now disappeared the farmhouse has survived and been converted into a private house.

The Manor House on Hasland Green operated as a farm during the 19th and 20th centuries and at that time it was known as Manor Farm. In 1891 Joseph Metcalf, his wife Sarah and three of their daughters were living there. Joseph was a farmer who was said to have been born in Hasland. It is not known how long the Metcalf family resided there but in later years it was occupied by William Heathcote and his family. It is now a private dwelling.

Churchside Farm is on the westerly side of Churchside and for many years William Hall and his wife Ann resided there. William, who was born in Hasland, was said to be farming 20 acres of land. He is known to have resided there until his retirement at which time his nephew William Gilding took over the farm. William farmed there until his sudden death in 1917. In later years it was occupied by the Booth family and the farmhouse still survives today.

On Calow Lane there were known to be three farms. Hawkin's Farm was at the bottom of Hoole Street, Steven's Farm was opposite Ashfield Road and further down was Hall's Farm.

PEOPLE

Whilst looking through various directories, census and other records regarding Hasland, it becomes obvious that certain people had a great impact on the village. It must be realised that these individuals helped to make Hasland the place it is today. There were the influential people such as the clergymen, teachers, land owners and colliery owners. The skilled, consisting of the engineers, builders, joiners, stonemasons, black-smiths and shoemakers. Of course there were also the farmers, publicans and shop-keepers, not to mention all the ordinary families such as the miners, railway workers and labourers who made their homes in Hasland.

I have gathered here some of the families who made their mark on the village.

Thomas Hill, Canon of Lichfield, Archdeacon of Derby and Perpetual Curate of Hasland lived at Hasland Hall

Walter Thompson and his assistant outside his butcher's shop in Hasland c1939.
Photograph courtesy of Sybel Webb.

between 1851 and 1868 and it was during this time that he was responsible for opening the Stable School within it's grounds. He showed great interest in the education of Hasland children, as can be seen from the school log books, until he died in 1875.

George Albert Eastwood was a J.P. and had been Mayor of Chesterfield on three occasions. In 1905 he gave a large sum of money so that the Methodist Chapel which was on Chapel Lane could be extended. As a result the building was named The Eastwood Memorial Schools. In 1912 he purchased Hasland House and grounds and gave it to the Borough of Chesterfield for use as a park. This was in memory of his late father Edward Eastwood who was a native of Hasland and had previously resided on Chapel Lane.

Bernard Chaytor Lucas, attorney, bank director and landowner lived for many

Copping's shop c1924. Ivy, Edith, Margaret and Walter Copping.
Photograph courtesy of Mary Boden.

years at Hasland Hall. In 1914 the Village Hall was built in Eastwood Park at his expense, and it was then presented to the people of Hasland. He did this in memory of his parents Bernard and Louisa. He also erected the Alms Houses in 1924 in memory of his mother.

William Handby was born in Bolsover in 1839 the son of Joseph and Charlotte Handby. He was a master joiner and wheelwright, as was his father before him. He moved to Hasland just after 1861 with his wife Esther and their young daughter Jane. Soon after, however, Esther died at the young age of 33. He later married his second wife Catherine and they had a daughter Kate Elizabeth. By this time two of his brothers, Joseph and George had also moved, with their families, to Hasland. They too were following the family tradition and were both carpenters. By 1901 William, Catherine and their family were living at Ivy House on Handby Street, so it is quite possible that William and his brothers had built the houses in this street. William died two years later aged 64 years, and according to his will, he owned quite a lot of property at the time, apart from his personal estate, so he must have been quite a wealthy man. Unfortunately, he had no sons to carry on the family name.

The Hoole family seem to have originated from Williamthorpe. The first trace that I have found of them in Hasland is on the 1851 census when Samuel Hoole, his wife Ann and three of their children are living at Herne House Cottage. Samuel was a rail labourer and his son James an engine driver. Ten years later Samuel was

Hampton Street c1905.

Hampton Street 2002.

The shops, Mansfield Road, Hasland, 2002.

The Green, Hasland, 2002.

Hasland or Winsick FC c1912.
Photograph courtesy of Mary Boden.

Hoole Street lads c1933.
Back row: Harold Rhodes, Gilbert Rhodes, Fred? Rhodes, Fred Swift, Robert Wood.
Front row: Ernest Wright, Harold Holmes, Albert Woolgar, Harry Nottingham.
Photograph courtesy of Robert Wood.

Hasland Girl Guides, 1944.
Photograph courtesy of Jean Hazell.

Hasland Workingmen's Club reserves, then called Winswick Rangers 1947.
Back row: Tom Burton (referee), John Brown, Harry James, Joe King, Eric Hadley, Geoff Brown,
Harry Ashall, Wilf Dumelow (trainer).
Front row: Ray Ashall, Eric Dickenson, Alan Dumelow, Geoff Hatton.
Photograph courtesy of Harry James.

farming 3 acres of land and his son James was a journeyman joiner. By 1871 James was a master carpenter living on Mansfield Road with his wife Harriett and their five children. Ten years later on the census date Harriett is at home with their children, who are now nine in number, and James is at Bank Close House with his son Walter who at the age of 15 years is said to be a blacksmith s apprentice. It is probable that James and his son were just working at the house rather than living there. They were to have two more children, making a total of eleven in all, with varying occupations including carpenter, confectioner and school mistress. By 1901 James and Harriett were living on Hasland Road and his son Henry James and family were living on Hoole Street, so it is a distinct possibility that James and his sons actually built the houses in this street. James died in 1906 at Beech Farm, Hasland but his wife survived for another 27 years. Several of James sons carried on the trade of joiner until well into the 20th century.

John Meakin first appeared in Hasland in 1861 when he was living on The Green with his parents John and Charlotte Meakin. They originated from Bolsover. John junior was farming 81 acres of land and his father was then retired, having previously been a stone mason. Ten years later John had married Isabella Childs and he was a grocer and publican at the New Inn on Calow Lane. During these years they had four children who all died in infancy. They later moved onto Calow Lane after John had retired, presumably due to ill health, as he was still only a young man. They seemed to be very prosperous as they always had a servant, and when John died in 1885 he was said to be a gentleman and Isabella was said to be living on her own means. John died at Ashfield House, Calow Lane and it is most probable that Meakin Street was named after him. Isabella lived for another eighteen years, also dying at Ashfield House in 1898 aged 53 years. In her will she left her pony and harness to Henry Bark who was a farmer living at Park Farm at Chatsworth. She also left £25 to her trustee Arthur Saxton and £100 to the trustees of the Chesterfield and North Derbyshire Hospital. As she had no surviving children, the remainder went to numerous relatives such as nieces and nephews and the nieces and nephews of her late husband. A few months after her death there was a sale by auction at the Angel Hotel in Chesterfield. Included in the sale was Ashfield House, many of the houses on Meakin Street, some houses on Calow Lane, The New Inn, some houses in Grassmoor and also some land at Whittington. These were obviously part of Isabella's estate.

Arthur Saxton was born in 1848 at New Brinsley in Nottinghamshire. He came to Derbyshire with his family at quite an early age, as when he was only a boy he lived at Ling's Row in Clay Cross. At only 7 years of age he began work at Ling's Colliery in North Wingfield where he received 10p a day and worked 13 hours a day in opening and closing doors. After being a pony driver for some time he went into the stall at the modest age of 15 years. He had no schooling beyond a little education supplied to him by the village curate, and he received no training until he attended technical classes at Chesterfield. He came to live in Hasland after marrying Martha Hoades who was also of Clay Cross. They had a son and

Hasland Methodist Church Youth Club Football Team 1957.
Back row: Peter Hollinshead, Charlie Heaton, Keith Hollindale, Philip Holleworth,
Malcolm Hollindale, Dave Sharratt, Gary Chance, Herbert Wall.
Front row: Ralph Hazlehurst, Graham Hartshorn, Jim Hall, Alan Pearce, Brian Mulroy.

Hasland Cricket Club 1960's.
Back row: Harold Davidson (Pop), Terry Conroy, John Hare, Graham Hartshorn, Rex Sleaman,
Ashley Calvert, Arthur Green
Front row: Bill Jowett, David Hall, Ken Green, Geoff Calvert, Peter Hole.

daughter, but, as many other people did at this time, they also lost three children in childhood. Whilst in Hasland, Arthur took a great interest in the Primitive Methodist Church of which he became a local preacher. He was also superintendent of the Sunday School for 20 years. Few men were better known in the mining world as all his working life was spent underground. He was under-manager for 35 years at the Black Shale Pit of Grassmoor Colliery Company. His wife Martha died in 1906 and two years later he married Miss Ellerker of Knaresborough. In public work he was certainly one of Hasland's leading representatives for many years. He was also a member of the Chesterfield Board of Guardians and the Rural District Council, and was chairman of the latter body in 1911. He left Hasland and moved to Matlock in October of the following year and of course resigned all his public appointments. He was still a frequent visitor to Chesterfield however, and in 1915 the Board of Guardians paid tribute to his work as an old miner by electing him a co-optive member. Matters affecting the welfare of miners were always warmly supported by him and he was one of the first members of the Midland Miners Fatal Accident Relief Society and in the absence of Mr A. G. Barnes, The President, he presided at many of the meetings. After he moved to Matlock he was not long before he returned to public work. He was a member of the Matlock Military Tribunal and of the Haddon Hospital Committee. He secured a seat on the Matlock Urban District Council in 1913, a position he held up to the time of his death. He died in 1917 at Brook House in Matlock at the age of 70 and was buried at Hasland Cemetery with his first wife Martha. A year later a marble tablet was unveiled in his memory at Hasland Methodist Church. There is also an identical one in memory of his wife Martha on the opposite wall which presumably was donated after she died which reads 'She laboured much for this church. Erected in grateful remembrance by her loving co-workers'. I am sure that many people, like myself, have sat in this church over the years and read the tablets little realising what an interesting story lay behind them.

BUILDINGS

HASLAND OLD HALL

The Old Hall was situated on the corner of Calow Lane and Chapel Street in Hasland, but there seems to be no reliable evidence to substantiate various theories as to the history of the building. However, I have gathered here some accounts from various sources regarding the Hall.

In the New Figaro Magazine of 1915 there is an article which reads 'We shall notice a once palatial building at the corner of Chapel Yard. This is the Old Hall or Manor. Here lived for some time John Linacre, brother to Thomas Linacre the celebrated scholar, who gave his name to the locality known as Linacre Woods, Old Brampton. John Linacre died in 1488. When the Civil War broke out in 1644 the Old Hall was the residence of Captain Roger Molineux, the redoubtable and gallant defender of Bolsover castle, when that stronghold was attacked. Captain Molineux sold the Hall to Captain John Lowe of Alderwasley.'

For many years it was divided into three dwellings, two on Calow Lane and one on Chapel Street but it was still referred to as Hasland Old Hall.

In 1950 Mr F. W. Davidson, who was then about 85 years of age, recalls being sent to Bridget Smith's shop, which was situated in part of the Hall, to buy some yeast when he was about 4 years old. He says 'We never looked upon the building as being anything more than what we were always told, that it belonged to the old coaching days. Everything points in that direction. How far back no-one seems to know. All the old coach buildings were in ruins before my Father's time.' Of his recollections of the building as it was in 1870, Mr Davidson said 'The Chapel Lane entrance opened into a T-shaped room, narrow at the beginning, then widening out with settles fixed to the wall. This entrance, in my idea, was for third class passengers and coachmen. The Calow Lane entrance was more decorative, with a porch entrance for first class passengers. On the other side of the road there was stabling, a very large thatched bungalow, and a well for the watering of the horses. The Hall itself is very attractive and pleasant to look at with it's sharp gable ends and it's stone-laced door and window frames, but all the glories and beauties of ancient buildings are missing. There are no gargoyles, corbels, fluted stonework, courtyard, paddock, outbuildings or garden. It is just built on the roadside corner. There was no sanitary or waste system from the Hall. In fact all the inhabitants of Hasland in those days had to carry their water from wells or springs. To mention three, Sick Well (at Manor Farm), Holywell (at the bottom of Grass Hill), and Gorse Field (in Calow Lane.)' Mr Davidson's Father and Mother were both employed by the Lucas family who lived at Hasland Hall.

Mr Thomas Anthony Cope bought the Hall for £300 early in the 20th century. He was the manager of Woodheads shop in Hasland at the time, and also lived at a shop which was on The Green next to Coppings shop. It seems that he bought the Hall mainly for sentimental reasons. His second wife, whose maiden name was Mabel Smith, was a native of Hasland. She had many childhood memories of the house in Calow Lane and was delighted when her husband bought it.

In the 1950's a tenant of the house who had lived there for many years, said that before a new fireplace was fitted in her living room, there was a coat of arms on plasterwork on the chimney breast. She made numerous enquiries to try to identify the arms, but without success. She believed that it had the date 1665 and the initials R.S. above it. She also said that the now disused third storey of the building had signs of oak panelling on the walls, an indication of grander days perhaps.

When the last part of the Hall was being demolished in 1984 a former tenant said 'How sad I feel when I look at what is left of the Old Hall at the corner of Calow Lane, Hasland, Chesterfield. It is now being demolished to make way for houses. I agree we must move with the times but this building was steeped in history. The question is, why wasn't it renovated and preserved? I did enquire some 28 years ago about the Hall's future, when the back of the Hall collapsed. The answer I got then was that no money was available. I know what I am talking about because when the Hall was made into three houses, I lived in one of them and brought up a family there. To begin with, it was an old coaching hall. It's even said that Ann Boleyn stayed there on her way to be beheaded. There were three or four tunnels running from the Hall, one to the Priory at Spital, one to Hardwick Hall, one to the oldest part of Hasland Hall School and one to the Crooked Spire. The fireplace was another feature. It was very large and if you looked up you could see openings in the chimney which had doors on. These seemed to be alternate doors on either side. I suppose robbers used them as hiding places. There was a beautiful crest over the large mantelpiece and on this crest was some coat of arms, consisting of a unicorn, oak leaves and acorns, a magpie and a lion. It was taken by a workman and given to an organisation in Chesterfield. The Hall had quite a number of windows which had been sealed up because of the window tax. The walls were two feet thick and the beams in the ceiling were the same. There was a second floor that we could reach by a trap door. Up there was a large room, the stone floor covering all the room. It had a large stone spit in the centre where the meat was roasted. Laths and lime were mixed together for insulating the walls. No nails were used, only hand-made pegs to keep things in place, and all the doors were beautifully carved with flowers and leaves in the heaviest oak panelling. Believe it or not we had a ghost too, a very friendly one. I saw a very tiny lady twice and my daughter saw her once. We got used to hearing footsteps and doors open. We took it all in our stride. I know it s too late to do anything about it now, but why didn't someone step in and try and preserve the heritage that Hasland owned and save this wonderful Hall? I'm sure many of the older people who knew it would share my views.

The Old Hall was subsequently demolished and several garages were built on part of the site. Later, a row of town houses were also erected on the Calow Lane side of the site where the front of the Hall stood. I have to agree with the comments which were made by the lady previously mentioned, when she said that it was a great pity that no-one had the foresight to attempt to save this building before it was too late.

THE MANOR HOUSE

It is not known exactly when the Manor House on Hasland Green was built, but parts of it are believed to date from the 15th or 16th century. At one time the house was called Farland Hall and it is believed that at some time it was moated.

The Great Hall still survives today although it is now divided between two storeys. A beam is visible on the first floor with a splendid carved foliate boss of 15th century date. A very old door still survives on the ground floor and there is also an ancient fireplace which is still in use.

Several years ago, the floor of the Great Hall was taken up by the present owners due to damp, and stone flags were found beneath it which were removed. A circle could be seen in the centre of the room, where presumably, the original fires had been many years before.

The Manor House was let as a farm during the 19th and 20th centuries. On the census it is difficult to ascertain who was actually residing at the Manor House as there were many farmers living on The Green in Hasland at that time. However,

An ancient door in the Manor House, Hasland.

Joseph Metcalf was leasing the farm late in the 19th century and by the early 20th century the Heathcote family were residing there.

There have been many stories told locally over the years, which said that at one time there was a footpath leading from the Manor House, across the fields towards Chesterfield, which led to Spital House. This was said to be a very ancient route.

Although not a lot is known about the Manor House, parts of it are certainly very old. It is at present a private dwelling.

Manor House Farm 1950's.
Photograph courtesy of Sue Ervine.

The Manor House 2004.

HASLAND HALL

The name 'Hasland Hall' is mentioned in various old documents, but it is not clear whether this refers to the site of the present building. However, it is believed that the oldest part of the Hall which still stands today was erected in about 1800. It was described as a stone and brick building of Georgian type which was in the centre of well-wooded parkland, 350 feet above sea level and perfectly screened from the main roads. It was approached from these roads by well-constructed carriage drives. There were also two lodges, one which stood at the entrance from The Green and the other at the Mansfield Road entrance. There were also a number of small buildings and cottages on the estate.

At the time of the 1851 census the Hall was unoccupied, but in 1861 there were only three people said to be actually residing there at the time. These were Thomas Smith who was said to be a gardener who was unable to work, his wife Mary Ann who was a laundress and their 18 year old daughter Julia Ann. At this time, presumably living in the coachman's house was James Dumelow, who was coach-man to the Venerable Thomas Hill who was Cannon of Lichfield, Archdeacon of Derby and Perpetual Curate of Hasland. The Reverend Thomas Hill is known to have resided at the Hall during this time until 1868 when he had a house erected next to St. Paul's Church in Hasland. However by 1871 the house was well occupied as Bernard Lucas, the Banker and J.P. had moved in, and he, together with his family and a variety of servants resided there for at least twenty years. By 1901 Charles Markham was residing there and on the 1901 census he had two visitors, these being Roy McGregor Lauri and the Hon. R. W. Chetwynd, who were both shipbuilders. There were also numerous servants there at that time too.

By 1930 the Borough of Chesterfield had put a three year scheme in place for the development of education in the district, and a proposal was made that they purchase

Hasland Hall in the 1930's shortly after it became a school. Taken from Hasland Hall Park which is now Broomfield Avenue and Hillcrest Road.
Photograph courtesy of Bill Ervine.

and reconstruct Hasland Hall for use as a Modern Mixed School to serve the Hasland area. Enquiries were made as to the risk of subsidence in the Hasland Hall grounds owing to the working of coal seams from Grassmoor Colliery in the immediate neighbourhood. However, the building only had one very small crack in it, and they were reassured that if additions to the Hall were specially constructed to avoid damage by subsidence, it would be possible for it to be used for this purpose. Consequently in May 1931 the Education Committee accepted the tender of Mr C. E. Gaunt of Chesterfield, amounting to £5,632, for the conversion of the Hall into a Senior School, and it's decision was subsequently confirmed by the Town Council.

Hasland Hall was opened as a Senior Mixed School in January 1932 thus concluding it's use for over 100 years as a private dwelling.

THE COTTAGE

I am sure that many people do not realise the age of The Cottage on The Green, Hasland. It is believed that the first part of the building was erected around 1659 by Francis Hardy. There is a stone, now set in a wall in the rear garden which has the engraving 1661 F.H. This could well be the previously mentioned Francis Hardy. On the William Senior Survey Map of 1631 there is a 'Francis Hardy' living just beyond Hasland Green on the Grassmoor Road. This is thought to be the site of The Cottage.

It is known that in 1827 Mrs Ann Lowe (nee Belfitt) was renting the property from William Waller. She was the widow of Thomas Lowe Junior who was a mill-wright from Nottingham. Thomas and Ann were actually cousins and their family originated from Old Brampton. Ann's father Samuel Belfitt was born in Old Brampton in 1757 and by 1797 he was living in Walton and was part-owner of a mill at Holymoorside, before moving to Nottingham where he died in 1817. Thomas and Ann's nephew, Thomas Lowe Acton, was about eight years old when he drew a sketch of The Cottage, and to this day the drawing is still in the possession of his grandson.

By the time of the 1841 census Robert Nall and his wife Elizabeth were living at The Cottage. Elizabeth pre-deceased her husband when she died in 1872, and Robert died two years later. They were both buried in the churchyard at St. Paul's Church, Hasland. During the time which they spent at The Cottage Robert was said in 1851 to be a cattle dealer occupying 22 acres of land , and in 1871 a farmer of 100 acres and landowner. They also had one male servant acting as a groom and servant of all work and one female house servant.

By 1881 William Waller and his wife Hannah had taken up residence at The Cottage and William was said to be a civil engineer and farmer of 14 acres. It is known that he originally served his apprenticeship to the first engineer of his day, the famous Robert Stephenson. He was the eldest son of William Waller who was Town Clerk of Chesterfield and Registrar of the County Court, who, in turn, was the son of Robert Waller, also Town Clerk of Chesterfield until 1791. William and

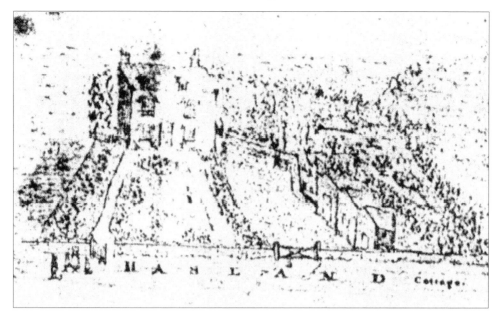

The sketch of The Cottage, Hasland, which was drawn by Thomas Lowe Acton in 1827.

Hannah continued to live at The Cottage until William's death in 1890, and Hannah then stayed there until her own death some twenty years later in 1910. It is presumed that Joseph and Phoebe Parker moved into The Cottage soon after the death of Hannah Waller. Joseph was born in Duckmanton and was a farmer. He and his wife Phoebe had five children Rebecca Elizabeth, Sarah Ann, William T., Francis A. and Florence Mary. Joseph died in 1937 and Phoebe lived another three years until 1940. Two of the Parker sisters remained at The Cottage after their mother's death and during this time they had it divided into two separate dwellings in which they could live separately. However after the death of the sisters the house was sold in 1968 at a public auction at the Hotel Portland in Chesterfield. It was described as follows. 'A superb small Georgian house in a beautiful setting within lovely grounds bounded by a wealth of fine timber. Completely detached from the surrounding residential area and having a unique position with extensive views over the countryside. Imposing front elevation with two large bow windows and built of stone and brick with part stone and part slated roofs. Wrought iron entrance gates lead to circular drive at the front of the residence with a broad central lawn having two Grecian style vases on plinths. The front of the property is screened by a wealth of fine timber of chestnut, oak, hawthorn, sycamore and other beautiful trees. The second entrance is to the carriage house'. It appears that The Cottage had lost none of it's charm since young Thomas Acton Lowe drew his sketch in the early 19th century.

Although the house has been extended a couple of times over the years it still has many of it's original features and to this day retains it's Georgian beauty.

HASLAND HOUSE AND EASTWOOD PARK

The history of Hasland House seems to be rather vague. There are various accounts regarding the building but I have chosen to quote from a report which was in The Courier newspaper at the time of the opening of Eastwood Park.

'Hasland House has a history which is lost in the past. It is a picturesque old place, and no-one who has passed through Hasland about Easter-Time can have failed to have their attention attracted to the grounds. For several weeks every year the fields, which can be seen from the road are carpeted in blue and purple by the crocuses which overrun the space, and to the present generation Hasland House is known more on account of it's blue crocuses than for any other reason. Who built Hasland House? We have inquired in likely quarters and the result is that no-one seems to know who built the place, or at any rate, who built the original portion, for it seems to have been added to on a number of occasions. It is a delightful old building, three-storied, surrounded by some fine old trees, and with a nice old-fashioned flower and kitchen garden. Then there is a tennis lawn which was made by the last occupier Mr Eric D. Swanwick, and the two fields together extend to about 15 acres. The smaller of the two has been used of late years as the cricket ground of the Hasland Church Institute Cricket Club. The first owner of Hasland House who is remembered by Chesterfield people today was the late Mr Josiah Claughton, who, in the middle of the last century, was an eminent wholesale chemist in Chesterfield. His business premises were on Low Pavement, on the West side of the entrance to the old Three Tuns Inn, but the business died out with the demise of Mr Claughton himself. Hasland House however was not built by Mr Josiah Claughton. The first part of it is probably 150 years old and almost entirely built of

Eastwood Park celebrations to mark the end of World War One in 1918.
Photograph courtesy of Stella Moseley.

The Village Hall, Hasland. Celebrations to mark the end of World War One in 1918.
Photograph courtesy of Diane Sheppard.

The Village Hall, Hasland. Celebrations to mark the end of World War One in 1918.
Photograph courtesy of Diane Sheppard.

brick. In the Chesterfield mind Hasland House is closely associated with the name of Claughton, as it was occupied for many years by four daughters of Mr Claughton, and there are, alive today, people who were in the service of those ladies when in residence. However, one by one they passed away until the holding became the sole property of Miss Catherine Claughton who died in the year 1895. By her will she bequeathed the house to her nephew the Reverend John Beedham, Rector of Bridgnorth. Shortly after this time the Rev. gentleman resigned his living and came to reside at Hasland House. Many older residents doubtless remember the sturdy figure of the Reverend gentleman as he moved about the village, for he soon became well-known in the place. He however did not live long to enjoy his inheritance, and he left a widow and one son. Mrs Beedham continued to reside at Hasland House but it was not very long before she too passed away, and the property passed to her only son John Arthur Beedham, who had been engaged in the Dominion for a good many years. Upon the death of his mother, Mr Beedham came over to England, but as his interests were more in Canada than the old country, he decided to dispose of the property. It was put up for auction in 1904 and the purchaser was the late Mr Bernard Lucas. It is from the trustees of Mr Lucas that Alderman Eastwood purchased the park.'

Alderman George Albert Eastwood of Brambling House, Hady was a J.P., had been Mayor of Chesterfield on three occasions, and was a very well-known figure in the Town. In the year 1912 he made it known that it was his intention to present the Town with Hasland House and grounds, for the purpose of a park which would be open to the public 'free and forever'. This was in memory of his father Edward Eastwood who was a native of Hasland and also a well-known benefactor.

During the following year the area was prepared for public use and on July 2nd 1913 the house and park were ceremoniously handed over. The Town Council were very grateful and decided unanimously that it would be fitting to further mark the date by admitting Alderman Eastwood an Honorary Freeman of the Borough. A special meeting of the Town Council was held in the Council Chamber at the Stephenson Memorial Hall in Chesterfield. After the ceremony was completed a procession was formed and they proceeded on foot to Hasland. The police took the lead, and the fire brigade with the motor-engine and steamer brought up the rear. Walking with Chief Constable Kilpatrick was the Mace Bearer Mr Paul Bradley, followed by Hasland Band and various public representatives. Large crowds lined the route of the procession and the whole of Hasland was decorated for the occasion. On arrival at the entrance to the park, the gates were opened by Alderman Eastwood's niece Miss Blanche Eastwood, with a golden key which had been handed to her by the Mayor. A small girl, Dorothy Knight, was chosen to present her with a bouquet and the party, followed by the large crowd of people which had assembled, then moved through the park to a flower-decked platform. Nearby was the ornamental fountain which had been donated by Alderman Charles Paxton Markham. This had previously stood in the grounds of his home at Ringwood Hall. Mr William Hancock aged 75 years, who was at that time the oldest male inhabitant

The entrance to Eastwood Park, Hasland.

of Hasland, presented Miss Eastwood with a gold casket which had been purchased with the money obtained from voluntary subscriptions made by the people of Hasland. This was followed by speeches from the various dignitaries who were present. Afterwards a number of guests were entertained to tea in a large marquee by Alderman Eastwood, whilst the children were entertained to various amusements in the grounds and to tea in their respective schools. The entertainments in the park consisted of music which was provided by the Chesterfield Town Silver Band, the Hasland Silver Band and the Bryan Donkin Orchestral Society. It was a great occasion for all the residents of Hasland at the time and great crowds of people remained in the park enjoying the festivities until dusk.

I am sure that many people who, like myself grew up in the village, will have many happy memories of time spent in Eastwood Park, as it has proved to be a very popular place over the years. There have been many recreational activities held there such as tennis, bowls, putting, cricket and football. For many years there have been swings, slides and roundabouts too. Football is still regularly played in the park but the Hasland Cricket Club ceased to exist quite a few years ago. There have been many fetes and galas held there including the Hasland Gala which was held for several years and was a very happy occasion. Many years ago a 'Young Farmer's Rally' was held there each year. It would be opened by someone famous who was most likely connected to farming, or, as I remember on at least one occasion, by one

Hasland House and the Village Hall, 2004.

of the characters from the radio series 'The Archers'. There were also animals such as cows and sheep, and tractors and farm machinery were on display.

Eastwood Park still appears to be at the centre of village life and in eight year's time is due to celebrate it's Centenary.

THE VILLAGE HALL

The Village Hall was built in 1914 just before the outbreak of the First World War. It was presented to the inhabitants of Hasland by Mr Bernard Chaytor Lucas. Mr Lucas had spent many years of his early life living at Hasland Hall, but in 1914 he was living at Clifton near Bristol. He had the plans prepared by Mr Roland W. Paul, an architect from Bristol.

The building was formerly opened on Wednesday 22nd July 1914 and, as Mr Lucas was unable to attend, the ceremony was performed by his sister Mrs Bethune.

The Mayor and Mayoress, Alderman and Mrs E. Shentall and around 500 guests attended the opening and enjoyed afternoon tea on the lawn at the rear of the caretaker's house. Hasland Band played a selection of tunes and the Brookside Quartet Party also gave several items.

Afterwards the guests, including a large number of Hasland residents, assembled in front of the new Village Hall where the Mayor and Mrs Bethune stood under the porch in the main entrance. The Mayor, on behalf of the Corporation of Chesterfield and the people of Hasland, asked Mrs Bethune to declare the Hall open. He asked her to accept, as a memento, a gold key, which was engraved with the Borough Arms. It was inscribed 'Presented to Mrs Bethune on her opening the Hasland Village Hall – 22nd July 1914.' Mrs Bethune then expressed her thanks to the Mayor for the key and formerly declared the Hall open.

In a report from the local press it was stated 'Hasland's happiness appeared to be complete last year when Alderman George Eastwood gave them the beautiful Eastwood Park, and on Wednesday the handsome Village Hall, which has been presented to the inhabitants by Mr Bernard Chaytor Lucas was formerly opened. The Hall, which is in itself a handsome building, situated right in the heart of the most glorious surroundings of Eastwood Park, will satisfy a long felt want in the South Ward of the Borough of Chesterfield. The residents of Hasland have for some years been without a hall wherein social and educational gatherings might be held, and as a consequence they had to content themselves with the limited accommodation provided by the various religious bodies. The new Village Hall is to be used for the inhabitants, without regard to political or religious faith and is sure to prove a real boon.'

Hasland Village Hall, pensioner's party. (Date unknown.)
Photograph courtesy of Harry James.

Over the years the Village Hall has been used for a variety of social gatherings such as school concerts, dances and wedding receptions. It was also a meeting place for the Old People's Club and it has been used as a baby clinic for at least 40 years.

It is still well-used by various organisations as it has been continuously since it was built.

PENMORE HOUSE

Penmore House originally stood at Buntingfield in Ashover. It was owned by John Bunting who, after he retired from his business as a mercer, had a wine and spirit store in South Street in Chesterfield. He decided that he needed to live nearer to Chesterfield, so around 1818 he demolished his Ashover house, carted it stone by stone, and re-built it at Penmore in Hasland. He and his family then resided at Penmore House, as it was then known, for several years. His wife Sarah died on 22nd December 1861 aged 96 years and John survived his wife by less than a fort-night as he died on 1st January 1862 also at the age of 96.

For many years after the death of John Bunting the house was occupied by the Misses Elizabeth and Hannah Eyre who were the sisters of Joseph Eyre who was a

Penmore House, Hasland, 2004

timber merchant living on Lordsmill Street in Chesterfield.

In 1900 Penmore House and the surrounding land was for sale by auction at the Angel Hotel in Chesterfield. It was described as a desirable family residence situated at Hasland near Chesterfield and was said to be within ten minutes drive of the Railway Stations. The description from the sale catalogue reads 'The house stands within it's own grounds and is a most convenient residence for a gentleman whose business requires him to be within easy distance of Chesterfield. It contains a drawing room, dining room with a large bay window, breakfast room, entrance hall, front and back staircases, kitchen, scullery, larder or pantry, cellars, 7 bedrooms, 2 W.C's and a lavatory. The grounds are well laid out. There is a good orchard and the whole is beautifully wooded. The outbuildings comprise stables, coach-house, cow-houses, pigsty and there are the usual outoffices.' It was sold for £4,000 to Mr Fred Farnsworth.

Later, the house was bought by Dr. Peck who lived there until his death, after which it was occupied by his wife and daughters until 1937 when it came up for sale once more. At this time it was advertised as 'Penmore House Estate' as the sale consisted of four lots, the first being the house and out-buildings and the other three being plots of land. However at this time the house went unsold, being withdrawn at £1,850. The plot of land on the North side of the house, consisting of 7,230 square yards was subsequently sold privately.

At the present time (2005) the building is used as offices.

BANK CLOSE HOUSE

It is believed that Bank Close House was built around 1830.

By 1851 it was occupied by William Drabble, his wife Elizabeth and his step-daughter Eliza Penelope Clay. They had three servants and a groom living with them at that time.

William was a solicitor and was in partnership with William Waller at their offices in New Square, Chesterfield. He was also Mayor of Chesterfield in the years 1853, 1854, 1856 and 1861. On the census of 1861 he was also said to be a Commissioner of Taxes, an Alderman and an Attorney.

It was during this time that a murder was committed at Bank Close House. In the intervening years Eliza Penelope had married Joseph Bright a wealthy landowner from North Wingfield. Joseph and Eliza were visiting Bank Close House one Saturday night in September 1868. At about 10 o'clock in the evening, George Kelk, who was Joseph Bright's coachman, and Holmes who was William Drabble's butler, heard a noise outside. They went to investigate and caught the man concerned, but during the struggle George Kelk was stabbed and died almost immediately. He had been Joseph Bright's coachman for some time and was said to be 'universally respected'. He was buried in the churchyard of St.Paul's Church, Hasland, and his headstone reads 'George Kelk of Old Coates, Notts. died 26 September 1868 aged 30 years while on the discharge of his duties, met with a sudden and cruel death in this parish. The stone was erected by his late Master and mistress of Nether Hall, Hathersage.'

By 1871 William's wife Elizabeth had died, but at the age of 78 years he was still said to be an Attorney in Practice and a Landowner. By this time his step-daughter Eliza Penelope, her husband Joseph and their three year old daughter Helen Grace, were all living at Bank Close House, together with a number of servants including a coachman, housemaid, nurse and charwoman.

William died in 1874 at Bank Close House, and at the time of the 1881 census Joseph Bright, his wife Eliza Penelope and their two daughters Helen Grace and Mabel Elizabeth were in Devon. They appear to have taken with them a coachman, governess and several servants. At this time Bank Close House was occupied by a housekeeper and kitchenmaid. James Hoole and his son Walter were also there, and as James was a master joiner and builder it is quite possible that they were working at the house whilst the family were away.

After the death of Joseph Bright in 1899 Eliza was still living at the house with her, as yet, unmarried daughters, and several servants including a 'useful lad' who I imagine could probably turn his hand to anything!

When both her parents had died and her sister Mabel had married, Helen Grace, still unmarried, continued to live at the house until her own death in 1946.

The Tube Works then bought the house which they owned until 1983. The following is a description of the house from the sale catalogue at that time:

'The house is an imposing Georgian-style stone-built residence believed to date back to the 18th century, standing in a privileged and elevated position in it's own extensive grounds, through which it is approached by a long and spectacular sweeping driveway which culminates in an excellent turning/parking circle. The house and stable block to the rear are listed as buildings of architectural and historical interest, the main house being Grade ll. Bank Close is a very rare anachronism offering superb spacious accommodation in a delightful setting within half a mile of Chesterfield town centre. Chesterfield Midland Railway Station is also conveniently situated within one mile of the property. Opposite the main entrance, across the enclosed courtyard, approached from the main driveway through the original stone gateway and piers, is an extensive stone range of out-buildings and stables being a listed building in it's own right. This block consists of a hay-store, stables, a loft, ostler's room/saddlery and a carriage house. To the right of the splendid tree-lined drive access, as one approaches from Hasland Road, an excellent area of natural meadow/grazing land extends down to the river Rother in respect of which there are riparian rights. There is also a delightful walled garden to the side of the main residence. The whole area which boasts an abundance of various mature deciduous trees extends to around four acres and there are excellent car parking facilities to the front of the house, the beauty of which is greatly enhanced by it's secluded natural setting.

After it was sold it was converted into an Old People's Nursing Home which is still it's use today.

HASLAND METHODIST CHURCH

Methodism was born in Hasland in the year 1831. After a lot of pioneering work and contacts, the first service was held in a cottage on Chapel Lane which belonged to Mrs E.Widdowson. This cottage is still standing today. However, as the number of members of the new Society grew, it was realised that more spacious and permanent premises were required.

Due to the efforts of two of the younger lady members, a moderate sized building, which stood near the entrance to Chapel Lane from the main Chesterfield Road, was taken over by the Society. This building was already ancient and had been used for a variety of purposes, the most recent of those being it's use as a shed in which a number of vehicles, of a type described as wool-pack wagons were stored. It needed quite a bit of cleaning and also had to be furnished and equipped as a place of worship, but it was soon converted into a small Chapel. In 1832 the Society became members of the Circuit, and came under the pastoral care of Reverend George Booth who had been appointed to the Circuit in the same year.

In 1842 the Society s tenure of the one-time wool-pack wagon shed terminated and the premises reverted once more to secular use as the village blacksmith's shop. Although remembered by older residents of Hasland this building has long since disappeared. Fresh premises for the Society now had to be found. This problem was overcome when the trustees purchased a plot of land, some stone from two farm buildings, and erected the first purpose-built Chapel on Chapel Lane. This would later become the Primary Department of the Sunday School. The building was constructed at a cost of £185 and it was estimated that it would seat about 350 to 400 people. This was known as the first Chapel and when it was first opened the lighting consisted of candles. There was also an inscription stone incorporated in the building, of which the engraving was done by the local schoolmaster of the time in his 'leisure hours'. He had a young assistant by the name of Obadiah Allen whose chief job was, it appears, to hold the candle, as most of his work was carried out by candle-light.

Eventually, a plot of land adjoining the first Chapel, which was the site of some old cottages, became available. Three of the stewards, who were also trustees, learnt of this only the evening before the sale was to take place, so there was no time to let the other members know about it. So, unknown to the remaining members of the Society, they proceeded to buy the land on behalf of the Church. Once the ground had been secured the members set about clearing the site themselves, therefore saving on the overall cost. By the year 1880 the work was complete and the stone-laying ceremony took place on 27th September. It was performed by Mr A. Barnes M.P. and in his speech he said 'One good result of the new Chapel would be that the friends would be able to devote the old building for the purpose of holding schools. At one time the Sunday School was the only means the working man had to give his child an education. But these times had altered, still the Sunday Schools had before it, work to perform, and they ought to prosper'. Sixty children connected with the Sunday School each laid a brick and the new Chapel then opened for public worship. This 1880 Chapel consisted of what was the lower portion of a two-storied building, the upper portion was added in 1905. This enlargement was made possible by a generous gift on the part of Mr G. A. Eastwood in the interests of the work of the Sunday School. The premises were dedicated in his memory as The Eastwood Memorial Schools .

During the following years plans and preparations were being looked at regarding the building of a third Chapel. So in April 1898, eighteen years after the opening of the second Chapel, an extensive plot of land was purchased on Hampton Street at a cost of £544. Mr W. Cecil Jackson of Chesterfield was engaged as the architect and he designed the new Chapel in the Gothic style. Mr R. Peck of Chesterfield was the builder. During the next two years a building scheme was adopted which involved an outlay of £2,700 and on August 15th 1900 the

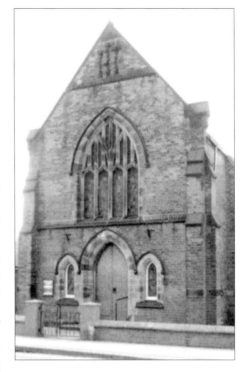

The Methodist Church, Hasland.

foundation stone-laying ceremony took place. Several prominent members of society were present including Mr Thomas Bailey M.P. for the Division, Lord Morpeth, Miss Bayley, Mrs C. P. Markham and Dr George Booth. Memorial stones inscribed with each person's name were also laid by, or on behalf of several other people who had donated subscriptions. By Good Friday of the following year the work was completed and opening services were held that day.

In 1986 discussions were held by the members of the Church due to the fact that the first and second Chapels, now the Sunday School rooms were in urgent need of major repairs. It was also becoming a problem that the Church and Sunday School were on separate sites. It was decided to extend to the rear of the Church on Hampton Street and this building was completed in April 1988. The opening ceremony took place on 14th May 1988 when a dedication service was held. Mr and Mrs Walter Jackson, the oldest members at the time, unlocked the door of the new building. In early 1988 the Sunday School premises were sold. They were cleared in March and the majority of the contents were sold to raise money for Church funds. The premises were finally vacated in April 1988 ending the Church's 146 year association with the site. This was a very sad occasion for many people as, for them, the building held many happy memories.

It is thanks to it's sound construction and continued maintenance that the present Church building is still as good today as when it was built over one hundred years ago. There is still a band of dedicated people there, who are willing to work very hard to ensure that Methodism remains in Hasland for many years to come.

ST. PAUL'S CHURCH

St. Paul's Church is situated on Churchside in Hasland. Prior to it's existence many of the inhabitants of Hasland would have been baptised and married at St. Mary & All Saints Church, namely the Crooked Spire, in Chesterfield.

The foundation stone was laid on February 21st 1850 by Archdeacon Hill who was presented with a silver trowel to mark the occasion. He then said 'I lay this stone in the name of the Father, Son and Holy Ghost, amen.' Three cheers were given, and then two copies of an inscription were deposited in a bottle which was let into the foundation stone, along with a shilling, sixpence and fourpence, which were silver pieces of the last coinage in 1846. The land had been donated by the Duke of Devonshire. It was said that 'The Church is to be built upon an eminence nearly opposite to Wingerworth Hall and commands an extensive view of the hills at Stonedge and Eastmoor, whilst further north, Sheffield can be discerned in the dim distance. It is to be built in the Elizabethan or Early English style. It is expected to be finished in November next. On the north of the Church a neat Parsonage House will be erected.'

The Church was duly built at a cost of £900, the architect being T. C. Hine of Nottingham. The builders were Rollinson and Heath of Chesterfield. It was said that 'The interior presents a beautiful and pleasing appearance and that in respect to convenience and comfort, no village churches can surpass it.' It was consecrated on September 24th 1850 by the Bishop of Lichfield in the presence of numerous clergymen and dignitaries. Apparently the day started out very gloomy and rainy but appeared to improve during the day. It was said that the Church, which would hold 230 people, would be opened on the Sunday following when the Rev. Valentine Green would be the preacher.

The first baptism to take place at the Church was of Selina Ann Parkin on June 9th 1851 when the officiating minister was George Butt. The first marriage was held on June 2nd 1851 and was between William Cooper and Sarah Roberts who were both of Hasland. The officiating minister for this marriage was Alexander Poole. The first burial to take place in the churchyard on October 13th 1851 was of Hannah Hollingworth the wife of Joseph Hollingworth who was a farmer living in Hasland.

By the year 1866 the Church was proving to be too small for the growing congregation and the north aisle was added at a cost of around £600. Messrs. Hoole and Handby carried out the work.

Some of the early Rectors of Hasland were The Ven. Thomas Hill, William Barnes, Horace Wilford, W. Vivian Davies, Cyril Norman Lavender, Alex Fraser and John Vaughan.

The following is an excerpt from a letter which was written by Mrs Adelaide Malcolm who was the daughter of the Rev. W. Barnes, on the occasion of the

St. Paul's Church, Hasland.

Centenary celebrations of the Church in 1950. 'It is the Church of my youth and always lovingly remembered by me. I think I had better talk about the old days as I remember them 75 or more years ago. Hasland then, was described as a hamlet, and the comparatively small population was composed chiefly of farmers and miners. The Midland Railway Co. had not then brought it's contingent of drivers and guards to occupy the rows of cottages called the 'Railway Cottages' and those on the hill. Archdeacon Hill lived at 'Churchside', the Squire, Mr Lucas, at the Hall. The three Misses Claughton at Hasland House. Someone before Mrs Waller (I quite forget the name) where Mr Parker now lives., and Miss Eyre at Penmore. The Church School was the only school, and the Archdeacon who built it, also the Church and the Rectory, was the first rector and my Father his curate. Between them they established a night school in the village which was much appreciated, and I remember hearing that the miner's leader, Mr Haslam, or was it Herreys, acknowledged that he acquired most of his education from that source. He then lived in a small cottage near the blacksmith's forge, but later he became quite an important person in the miner's union, I think it was, and a large house was built for him in Saltergate, Chesterfield. Some of you may remember seeing Mrs Hill, the Archdeacon's wife, being wheeled about the village in a bath chair. The Post Office was kept by Miss Widdowson and was just a cottage in the row above Hill's shop at the corner, and Miss Widdowson's front room was the office where all the postal business was transacted. Her rate of payment was assessed by the number of letters passing through her office, and certain days were chosen for counting them.

The Toll Bar was then in existence and all vehicles passing through had to halt and pay the toll. I forget the amount, very little probably, but it must have been a nuisance. Miss Claughton was able to avoid it, though I don't know that she ever did so, for she had one entrance to her drive just beyond the Toll Bar on the Chesterfield Road, and the other near the forge on the Mansfield Road. The Old Hall was, and probably still is, at the village end of Calow Lane and at one time was occupied by old Mr Lucas, the Squire's father.

I wonder how many remember the Sick Well. It was in a field just over a stile near the Policeman's cottage, probably one of the fields on William Hollingworth's farm. It was only a trickle coming out of the hillside and whether it really possessed any medical virtue or not, I can't say, but we looked upon it as second only to the Pool of Bethesda!!

At Hasland House there was a beautiful velvety lawn, and Miss Claughton once told us that she and her sisters made it themselves, not with sods, but by transplanting bits of fine grass all over it. I hope it is still there and kept in good order. They had a great friend, Miss Gratton, who lived with them and was like a sister to them. The Misses Claughtons were aunts of Miss Bright whom you will all remember with respect and affection. She and her sister lived such a quiet secluded life with their parents at Bank Close, that it has always astonished me how, in later life, she developed into quite a public character, taking an active part in so many organisations for the good of the parish and the district generally.

I remember the Archdeacon as a most saintly and very frail old gentleman in the true sense of the word.

In the days I am writing of, the Clay Cross Co. had not started the disfiguring colliery workings opposite the Rectory, and we had a clear view across the valleys to Wingerworth Hall, and often heard the peacocks there, when rain threatened. We enjoyed the immunity from smoke during the great colliery strike, and when all the pit ponies were brought up and put in the fields they were, for a time, blinded by the unaccustomed daylight.

I have told of my recollections of old Hasland and now I am wondering how many are left to recall with me those far off days. Though old age and infirmities prevent me from visiting it, the place is very dear to me and full of happy memories.'

The Lychgate at the entrance to the Church was erected in 1950 as a memorial to Miss Hannah Hollingworth who was, for 50 years, headmistress of the Church of England School in Hasland. The gate, designed by Maurice Wheatcroft, was made of oak and supported by a stone foundation. The roof of the gate was of hand-made tiles which, together with the stonework, was carried out by Arthur Carr and Sons and Alan Smith, builder of Hasland. The wood was carved by Alan Bramley of Wingerworth. The main organiser of the 'Lychgate Fund' was Thomas Cope of The Green, Hasland.

Hasland Church still has a very strong band of people who work tirelessly to maintain the reputation of their Church, which was built with such dedication more than 150 years ago.

WESLEYAN METHODIST CHURCH

The Wesleyan Methodist Church which was situated on The Green in Hasland was opened on 4th October 1899 by Miss Bayley who was from Lenton Abbey in Nottingham.

For many years the church seemed to prosper but by the year 1961 the members had decided to amalgamate with the Primitive Methodist Church on Hampton Street. It was decided that the name of the new church was to be 'The Methodist Church, Hasland'.

The last service was held at the Hasland Green Church on 26th November 1961 when both congregations took part in a united service. The preachers were Mr Alwyn Windle and Alderman L. Wilkinson. The congregation then walked round the corner to the Hasland Road Church carrying with them their pulpit bible. This was then placed on a new lectern by one of the church members, Mrs Moseley. Both the bible and lectern were dedicated by the Reverend D. A. Wollen, the Circuit Superintendent Minister, who was there to greet them. Sister Elizabeth Gillings was to have charge of the united Church.

The two Sunday Schools, which had previously been joined together, were being held in the Schoolrooms on Chapel Lane.

The original church building still stands today and after being used to accommodate various businesses over the years, it is at the present time unoccupied.

HASLAND BAPTIST CHURCH

A small group of people formed the first Baptist Church in Hasland in 1912. They met in a corrugated iron building which was situated on Eyre Street which became known affectionately as the 'Tin Tab'. Over the years this building was also used by several other organisations, but after a while became too small for the growing Baptist congregation.

In 1936 it was decided to build a new Church and a plot of land was purchased on the corner of Kent Street and Eyre Street. This was only a few yards from the 'Tin Tabernacle'. The members worked very hard to raise the money to build the new Church, and the foundation stones were laid on a snowy Wednesday afternoon on 15th January 1937. These stones cost £5 each and were laid by Mr Priestley, Mr I. McDonald, Mr J. H. Hadley, Mrs A. Clarke, Mrs Stevenson, Mr S. Stevenson and Mr A. Randall. Many of the other members laid bricks which were more modestly priced at 5/- each. Tea was served in the 'Tin Tab' and the Mayor of Chesterfield, Councillor G. F. Kirk, presided at the evening service. He congratulated the members on their work and said that he hoped they would go from strength to strength. The Reverend H. A. Harcup also spoke at the service.

The opening service was held on 3rd March 1937 when a large crowd gathered. The builder was Mr F. Durham of New Whittington and he handed the key to Mr Priestley who unlocked the door. The prayer of dedication was made by the Reverend J. H. Broadbelt of Cliff College who conducted the afternoon service.

Some of the friends who were present were Miss B. Eastwood, Miss Bright, Mrs Mark Hall, Mrs R. Stevenson, Mrs Mawhood, Mr T. W. Priestley President of East Midland Baptist Association, Mr H. Smith and Mr H. Spencer Cross Street Baptist Church, Mr G. Pattison Hasland Green Methodist Church, Reverend H. A. Haden President of D.C.E.M.B.A., who gave the address at the evening service, and friends from many other churches. The builder, Mr F. Durham, presented the Church with a communion table and several other gifts were given including a carpet. The organist for both services was Mr Billy Brailsford, and a vote of thanks to all who had helped to build the Church, was given by Mr Hewitt.

Over the years several alterations were made to the building including a stone entrance porch with toilets on the Eyre Street end, and a new stone vestry which was added to the rear end of the Church. However, by 1989 the building was requiring a lot of maintenance and the roof was in need of a lot of attention. It was decided therefore to consider the prospect of a permanent new building. After drawing up the plans, submitting them and getting the relevant planning permission, a building fund was started. The members worked tirelessly to raise the money for their new Church and it was finally opened on 14th September 1991. The Mayor and Mayoress, Councillor and Mrs Bill Jepson, were present at the service. The keys were handed over by Mr Paul Taylor, the building contractor. The door was unlocked and the ribbon cut by 90 year old Mr Albert Randall who had been Church secretary at the opening of the previous Church in 1937. He was assisted by Mr Henry Cox who was also one of the older members who had been present at the same occasion. A prayer of dedication was made by Mr Joe Smith who was a former Pastor, which was followed by the first service in the new Church.

The Church is still in use today and stands as a monument to the dedication of all it's members over the years.

HASLAND CEMETERY

By the year 1882 the churchyard at St. Paul's Church had become very full, so it was decided that a plot of land was to be found to provide a new burial ground. The Chesterfield Rural Sanitary Authority managed to secure from Mr B. Lucas J.P., a plot of land which was 5,724 yards square on the opposite side of the road to the church. The price paid for the land was £277 and it was estimated that the cost of preparing it for the purposes of burial would amount to about £1000. The whole expense was to be met by a loan repayable in thirty years. The contract for the buildings and for the laying out and draining of the land was let to Mr James Hoole of Hasland. There were to be no chapels on the ground, the only building being the caretaker's lodge, which was to be a substantial structure in the Gothic style. Mr Proctor, a nurseryman from Chesterfield, was to be entrusted with the planting of trees and shrubs. The cemetery was to be divided into two portions, consecrated and unconsecrated.

The cemetery was opened on February 7th 1883. A consecration service, performed by the Bishop of Lichfield, was held at St.Paul's Church the next day. The Reverends H. Cottingham, G. Butt, F. J. Metcalfe, J. J. Singleton, G. W. Darby, R. P. Hills, J. C. Massey, W. Dampier, S. C. Sarjant, R. T. Shee and R. Longworth were also present. After the service a procession was formed, headed by the church-wardens and representatives of the Rural Sanitary Authority, which proceeded to the burial ground. The procession then paraded around the ground repeating psalms and prayers and thereby consecrating the cemetery.

In 1907 it was enlarged, with a further two acres being added to the site.

The cemetery is still in use today and the cemetery lodge is still standing although it is now a private house.

PUBLIC HOUSES

At the present time there are five public houses in Hasland.

THE DEVONSHIRE ARMS

The present mock-Tudor building was erected in the 1930's. Prior to that the original building is believed to have been an old coaching inn complete with stables, which was previously known as the Devonshire Hotel. On both the 1851 and 1861 census the innkeeper was recorded as James Hancock who was born in Hasland. He was said to be an innkeeper and farmer so he must have led a very busy life. He was followed in 1871 and 1881 by George Fisher who originated from Ault Hucknall. In 1891 John James Hill, who was only 24 years of age at the time, was the innkeeper. He was also born in Hasland and was said to be a wagonette proprietor too, so presumably he ran his business from these premises. By 1901 Herbert Hollingworth had taken over the Devonshire Arms. Early in the 20th century Albert Edward Bell took over the license and, according to local tradition, he also ran a kind of taxi service in the area with his coach and horses.

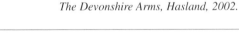

The Devonshire Arms, Hasland, 2002.

The Shoulder of Mutton, Hasland, c1900.

SHOULDER OF MUTTON

This public house seems to have had many proprietors over the years, these being John Mather from 1829 to 1851, Henry Windle in 1861, who was also a master carpenter and wheelwright, Richard Wheeldon in 1868, Charles Revill in 1871, William Ball in 1881 and 1891, and Reuban Hopkinson in 1901. In 1915 Jim Farnsworth died at the early age of 29 years of age after being the innkeeper at the Shoulder of Mutton for about 8 years. He was the son of Frederick Farnsworth who kept the Sportsman Hotel at Grassmoor for many years. There is the date 1913 engraved on the front of the building so it is possible that this was the year when the new frontage was constructed.

The Shoulder of Mutton, Hasland, 2002.

The New Inn, Hasland, 2002.

THE NEW INN, MANSFIELD ROAD, WINSICK

In 1871 Joseph Hawkins was residing here and he was said to be an innkeeper and coal miner. John Fletcher, who originated from Clay Cross had taken over this public house by 1881, and Richard Wood, who was also a coal miner was there in 1891. By 1901 William Casson who came from Billingly in Yorkshire was in residence. Early in the 20th century Wilfred Copping was licensee of the New Inn until in 1917 the license was transferred to his wife Alice as he was said to have 'joined the colours'. In later years Wilfred moved to the King's Head public house which was in Knifesmithgate in Chesterfield.

THE NEW INN, CALOW LANE

All the occupants of this public house appear to have been grocers as well as publicans. Joseph Taylor who was born in Staveley was the innkeeper in 1851 and he was also said to have 5 acres of land. By 1871 John Meakin was the licensee and he was followed by David Bedford in 1881 and Henry Broadhead in 1901.

The New Inn, Calow Lane, Hasland, c1900.

THE WINSICK ARMS

This was originally a private house named Birchill Lodge which was owned by the Grassmoor Colliery Company. Apparently it was quite a large attractive building with beautiful gardens. At some time after 1921 it was changed into a public house which was named the Telmere Lodge. A few years ago it was re-named as the Winsick Arms.

ALMS HOUSES

The Alms Houses were erected in 1928 in the centre of Hasland opposite the shops. Their official name was the Louisa Lucas Memorial Homes, due to the fact that they were erected by Mr Bernard C. Lucas in memory of his mother who had died some years before. Mr Lucas was a J.P., bank director and landowner and for many years lived at Hasland Hall.

It was said that the houses were to be occupied by 'couples of advanced age who have reached the twilight of their lives without attaining a bountiful share of the world's goods'. All the occupants had to be natives of the parish of Hasland.

The design and arrangement of the block was prepared by Messrs. Clayton and Rignall, architects, of Corporation Street in Chesterfield. The block comprised of five separate dwellings which consisted of 'a snug living room, an attractive little bedroom, scullery, larder, coal shed, etc.' The building was of the bungalow type and it was said to have had a pleasing external appearance which it still retained. The garden was simply and tastefully laid out, the lawn being interspersed with flowering cherry trees and surrounded by a golden privet hedge.

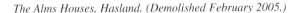

The Alms Houses, Hasland. (Demolished February 2005.)

The houses were handed over to the Chesterfield Municipal Charity Trustees and they were to choose the occupants.

They were actually opened in December 1928 and the first occupants were Mr and Mrs John Riggott of Mansfield Road, Mr and Mrs Joseph Butler of Storforth Lane, Mr and Mrs W. Preater of Hampton Street, Mr and Mrs James Simpson of Storforth Lane and Mr and Mrs G. Cox of Calow Lane.

Due to continued damp which apparently could not be rectified, the Alms Houses have been demolished (February 2005) and are to be replaced by six bungalows. The residents have been relocated and are to be returned to the new buildings when they are completed.

THE CARLTON CINEMA

An application for a license in respect of a new cinema at Hasland was made on September 14th 1922 by Thomas Dawson Unwin. In addition to the usual cinematograph authority the license asked for, included permission for music and dancing. The Chief Constable offered no objection. They were new premises and while he had not, as then, inspected them, he understood that they were satisfactory. An application was granted for 14 days on the conclusion of which a formal application was to be made.

The new Picture House was formerly opened by the Mayor, Alderman W. Rhodes on September 18th and it was described as 'a substantial and well-built place, being a modern and up-to date structure with a pleasant interior, ample accommodation and every convenience for it's patrons.' The Mayor spoke of the educational value of good moving pictures and Alderman H. Cropper thanked him on behalf of the Directors and said that it remained to be seen whether the people in the district desired a Picture House in their midst. The manager was Mr T. D. Unwin.

The first film to be shown at the new cinema was 'Married Life' which was said to be a comedy with a West End cast. This ran from the opening night until Wednesday, followed by 'The Golden Hope' featuring Edith Storey, which was showing until the end of the week. Of course there was also the 'News in Pictures' which was showing every night too. There was a matinee on Saturdays at 2.30pm which was 'for children only'. Seats could be reserved at the cinema and the price of admission was 1s 6d which included tax!

Soon after the opening of the cinema a party of children from the Hasland Junior School was taken there to hear a lecture on 'China'. There were several other visits over the years by the children, with lectures on subjects such as 'The Empire' and 'Paper and Cardboard Making by Mr E. Robinson'. They were also taken there to see the film 'The Great White South'.

Over the years it proved to be very popular, but by 1958 attendances were dwindling and it was decided to close the cinema. Apparently at this time, many local cinemas were suffering a similar fate. Only the Lyceum at Whittington Moor remained, apart from the Regal, Odeon and Gaumont in Chesterfield town centre.

The Carlton Cinema finally closed it's doors on July 25th 1958 after 36 years of screen entertainment, and the last film to be shown was 'The Joker is Wild'.

The building still remains standing today and is now occupied by a tyre company.

HASLAND WORKINGMEN'S CLUB

The club was formed just after the turn of the century above a joiner's shop at the top of Calow Lane. The club at that time had a bagatelle table and sold only soft drinks. In their first year the total takings were approximately £40. The first barrel of beer was supplied by Brampton Brewery to these premises.

The club moved onto the present site at Hampton Street a few years later. Before the Second World War the average takings of the club were £40 per week and the membership approximately 250. The premises underwent an extension in 1939 to provide a concert hall at a cost of £2180. The members were asked to lend money at a reasonable rate of interest, and the amount required was easily forthcoming. Within four years the whole of the money borrowed had been repaid.

By 1952 the membership was 1,000 and the average takings were £280 per week. A sign of the times was that ladies were not allowed to become members. They were allowed as guests but always had to be accompanied by a member, preferably their husband! At that time they had a football team, a whist team and a billiards team. Every year an outing was arranged for member's children who were of 'school age'. There was also an annual outing for members who were 65 years and over, and each Christmas these older members were given 10/- each. If a member was unfortunate enough to have a long illness, he was sent to one of the club's convalescent homes for a fortnight free of charge, and was given £1.10s pocket money.

The concert hall was further extended and the club was entirely modernised some years later. Various other alterations have also taken place over the years.

In an article from 1977 it stated 'A pipe major of their own, a welfare fund which they believe is the only one of it's type in Derbyshire, and a tradition for providing Mayors of the Borough, are among the proud boasts of the Hasland Workingmen's Club and Institute. The pipe major, officially recognised by the club is Mr John Jock Pringle, a former Seaforth Highlander and a former world champion piper for three years in the 1930's. Jock of Penmore Street, appeared at the club on New Year's Eve last (1976), complete with kilt, bringing the flavour of the Scottish Hogmanay to the night's proceedings. A recent acquisition is a new organ and although the club does not have a resident organist, they have a resident drummer, Mr John Cronin, who has been beating out the rhythm for about 15 years.

The club's Welfare Fund, club President Mr Ralph Hooper believes, differs from others in the County because it is non-contributory. The Welfare Fund, which gets it's money from the sale of welfare tickets and a tote, provides senior members with a Christmas present and Summer Outing each year. About 200 members of the club are pensioners. The club can point to providing three Mayors of the Borough from among it's membership – Ald. George Heathcote and Councillors Vic Allen and Jack Ford. Wife of member Mr Henry Collishaw, Mrs Annie Collishaw, was also a Mayor. The club numbers a Government Minister among it's membership – Mr Eric Varley, M.P. for Chesterfield and Minister for Industry. The oldest member of the club is founder-member Mr Ernest Powell of Ashfield Road, now aged 99.

A matter of pride at the club is that the membership subscription has never altered throughout the club's history, working out at 20p per year or less if a member opts to pay for eight years membership.

The club has a truly local flavour because membership is confined to residents of Hasland. The club has a 21-strong committee and their President, Mr Hooper, is also the President of the Derbyshire Branch CIU. Mr Hooper, a Justice of the Peace, has completed 21 years on the committee of the club.'

The details of the club in 1977 were:

Name: The Hasland Workingmen s Club and Institute.

Address: Hampton Street, Hasland

Number of Members: 1,900 (1,500 men, 400 women)

Membership Fee: 20p plus VAT for one Year or £1 plus VAT for 8 years

Established: 1902

Some Bar Prices: Mansfield Bitter 22p, Alpine Lager 27p, Brandy 31p, Whisky 23p, Vodka 23p, Best Sherry 16p.

Over the years the club has been very much a part of the Hasland community and it is still in constant use today.

HASLAND LOCO SHEDS

Hasland Loco Shed was the Midland's Chesterfield Depot. It was situated on the East side of the Midland main line between Derby and Sheffield. It was a standard roundhouse and it's early history is complicated by the company's intermittent use of the alternative name 'Clay Cross'. There was a turntable which was installed at a cost of £893.18s 1d. and for many years the Shed operated without a roof, this being the result of a severe storm during Wintertime. Over the years it provided locos for passenger trains from Chesterfield Midland Station, and for coal trains to and from many local collieries such as Grassmoor, Williamthorpe and Holmewood.

With the opening of the shed in 1875 many families came to live in Hasland from various parts of the country, as can be verified by the census at this time.

Two rows of cottages named Loco Terrace were built next to the Shed, for the railwaymen and their families, therefore creating their own little community.

There were further rows of terraced houses built by the side of the railway line towards Storforth Lane. These were called Midland Cottages comprising of North Terrace, Railway Terrace, Midland Terrace and Traffic Terrace. These were also occupied by the railwaymen and their families, but of course many of the workers also lived in the centre of Hasland.

The Hasland Loco Shed was closed on 7th September 1964, the men having been previously transferred to the Avenue Depot further up the line. The crumbling remains of the Shed were then demolished, and in 1978 the houses in Loco Terrace were condemned and were also demolished at a later date. Today no sign of the Shed or these houses remains, however the Midland Cottages are still standing.

SCHOOLS

The first known school in Hasland was the Stable School which was founded between 1845 and 1850 by Archdeacon Thomas Hill who had been largely responsible for the opening of the Victoria Schools in Chesterfield at an earlier date. The Stable School was held in a room over the stables at Hasland Hall and was accessed by an outer staircase. The Mistress of the school was Miss Hannah Smith who could not have been more than nineteen years of age when she succeeded a Miss Gregory. Miss Hannah Hollingworth, who was later to become a teacher at the National Schools attended this school and said 'Miss Smith taught single-handed and was a young delicate woman, with the seeds of consumption in her system. Those big strong boys were not plaster saints, but required constant correction, and got it. Girls too were not spared. I know, I got my share and no doubt deserved it. It will be well understood that individual teaching was out of the question. I never remember being definitely taught anything except religious knowledge. What a jolly playground the old yard made, what splendid hiding holes were there. We had many visitors even at the old place, and first and foremost was the saintly old Archdeacon Hill. What a picture he was. His kind beautiful old face and his snow white hair, his gentle voice and courteous manner never failed to impress the younger and worst of us. No-one could be naughty in his presence, and I never remember anyone being so.' The old Stable School closed in 1864 when Miss Smith and the children migrated to the new premises on Hasland Green.

The foundation stone was laid in 1864 for the National Schools, now the Hasland Green School. The following is an excerpt taken from the report in the local press regarding this event 'The foundation stone of the Hasland National Schools was laid on Wednesday September 21st by the Ven. Archdeacon Hill. The building is intended to be built of wall stone from Wingerworth quarries and consists of a schoolroom to accommodate 120 children with classroom, outer porch and master's house attached, the design being early domestic Gothic. Ample provision is made for separate playgrounds with suitable sheds and conveniences at the back of the building, and the front will be laid out as a pleasure garden. The architect is Mr S. Rollinson of Chesterfield. It was completed and opened later that year. Miss Smith and the scholars were transferred there and she had just one assistant at that time. Pupils came from Hasland, Calow, Wingerworth and part of Chesterfield.'

Miss Smith died in 1874 at only 39 years of age after 20 years service to the school. On her epitaph in the churchyard of St. Paul's Church, Hasland it says 'This stone is erected by her pupils in grateful remembrance of the unceasing pains with which she instructed them, in the knowledge of all those truths which concerned their present and everlasting welfare.' She was obviously held in great esteem by the people of Hasland.

She was succeeded by Miss Martha Beaumont. It was during this time that Miss Hannah Hollingworth became a pupil teacher at the school. However, Miss Beaumont did not remain for very long, as it was felt that the school, with it's undoubted unruly element, needed the hand of a master. Mr Thomas Rowarth took charge in 1876 with his wife to help as sewing mistress. He found the children 'in great disorder but willing to obey.' However he only stayed until September 1877, so perhaps he found it all too much for him!

It was during this time that Archdeacon Hill made frequent instructional visits and the day after his death in 1875 the

Hannah Hollingworth, Mistress at the Hasland Church Infants School.
Photograph courtesy of Evelyn Hollingworth/

Misses Claughton from Hasland House visited the school to enquire the number of children in Day and Sunday School to put the children into mourning for him. The school closed on the day of his funeral as a mark of respect.

Thomas Rowarth was succeeded by Mr Isaac Major who was born at Habrough in Lincolnshire. His wife also acted as sewing mistress at the school. Mr Major was to stay in Hasland for the next ten years.

The log book entries are often apologetic for low attendances and some of the reasons given throw an interesting light on local conditions of both health and labour. In March 1891, for example many children left the village, having gone to reside at Blackwell. The Midland Railway Company had erected a new engine shed there, and they had transferred many of the Hasland drivers. Nevertheless, the village grew in numbers and such overcrowding took place in the school that in about 1886 the infants had to move for ten years to the Primitive Methodist Chapel.

In the Summer of 1895 an addition was made to the existing school building by extending the north part of the main schoolroom towards the road. However wet weather hampered the work and seriously interfered with the routine of the school. The master was forced to use the porches and he notes in August that 'for the past four weeks the lower part of the school has been left open to the sky. Rain has frequently fallen doing much damage'. At the end of August he added 'the added portion is at last fit for use, and the glazed partition is a great improvement'. During the following months a new brick school, south of the existing building, was built

The staff of Eyre Street School c1926.
Back row: Miss Hudson, Miss Cooper, Miss Ball.
Middle row: Miss Pickard, Mrs Dean, Miss Walton (Head), Miss Jackson, Miss Ball.
Front row: Miss Longden, Miss Heron.
Photograph courtesy of Jenny Lord, Eyre Street School.

Eyre Street School, 1930.
Photograph courtesy of Evelyn Hollingworth.

Eyre Street School 2003.

Eyre Street School, 1971

for the infants. It was opened for work on March 25th 1896 and there was accommodation for 198 children. To meet the expense, a new School Building Fund had been started. Further additions and improvements to the old building came gradually, such as central heating in 1909. But the greatest boon was the opening of Eyre Street School as a temporary school for juniors in 1904. It was officially opened by the Derbyshire County Council in March 1905. Until then the onus of Hasland education had fallen entirely on the Church. Nevertheless, the school was in effect condemned in 1912, but mainly due to the efforts of the Rector, the Rev. W. Vivian Davies, a large building fund was raised. In October 1913 the Headmaster reported that 'During the extended holiday the premises have been remodelled. Every window on the premises, with a single exception, is new. Swinging lights and hoppers afford adequate ventilation, while the area of glass has been nearly doubled. New cloakrooms and lavatories are provided. A corridor gives separate access to each room. Unfortunately, in the years that followed, natural structural deterioration set in once more. The worst feature was undoubtedly the defective heating system, and for weeks on end the temperature of the school was between 30° and 34°F. The historic eleven foot desks with their nine inkwells and seating accommodation for eight children were still in use. There were no backs to them, and the fact that this was an advantage to adult meetings, in that the desk tops could be turned over to form a shoulder rest, was in all probability very little comfort to the children who used them in the daytime.

It appears that there were still problems with the heating in the 1930's as it was stated that 'the present heating system is definitely defective and the new Headmaster of the school, Mr H. Keeton and his five assistants are no doubt thankful that the Winter of 1931-1932 was abnormally mild. Their difficulties were further eased by the fact that as the school has, since January 11th 1932, only accommodated junior children, the best classrooms alone have been used'.

The Hasland Eyre Street Infant's School was opened in March 1905 by the Derbyshire County Council as a Junior Mixed School. It was certainly not full as it only had 104 children on the roll and it had a maximum of 370 pupils. It was hoped eventually to start a nursery department for the younger children. The building consisted of one block with five classrooms to the left and right of a main corridor. At each end of the corridor was a staffroom, one for the Headmistress and one for her assistants. In 1910 the Borough Extension transferred the school to the Chesterfield Education Committee. The overcrowding at the Hasland Church of England School (Hasland Green School) necessitated the transfer of the Infant Department of 148 children to Eyre Street in 1921. The school was unable to accommodate this large number, so consequently a temporary school was held from January 1921 until August 1927 in the Primitive Methodist Schoolroom in Chapel Lane. Sixty of the youngest children were accommodated in this building. In 1927 the Eyre Street premises were enlarged by the addition of a wing at right angles to the main line of the original block, and the total accommodation of this enlarged Infant and Junior School was 412. During the Summer holiday of 1931 the

The staff of Hasland Junior School, 1950's.
Back row: Mr Esland, Mrs Langenus, Mr Roberts, Miss Pickard, Mr Morgan, Miss Haynes,
Mr Dunelow (caretaker).
Front row: Mr Fry, Mrs Bothwell, Miss Mason, Mr Greaves (head), Miss Weston, Miss Mullins,
Mr Owen.
Photograph courtesy of Joan Mullins.

premises, internally and externally were decorated by Messrs. Eyre & Sons of Chesterfield. In January 1932 Miss D. S. Goodwin was appointed as Headmistress and she was helped by five assistant teachers.

The opening of Hasland Hall as a Senior Mixed School at the beginning of January 1932 caused further changes. The old Church of England School became a Junior Mixed School and the transfer of the juniors enabled Eyre Street School to accommodate exclusively the infants of the Hasland district. Few changes in equipment were necessary other than the taking over of the desks suitable for juniors to the Church of England School, and the provision of a few kindergarten chairs.

It was with the sale of Hasland Hall Mansion House with cottages, farm buildings and lands in 1924 that the first steps towards the new school were taken. The second step was taken in 1931 when the Hall itself and surrounding gardens and parkland, approximately 12·75 acres in all, was sold to the Mayor, Aldermen and Burgesses of the Borough of Chesterfield.

In spite of difficulties and delays due to bad weather, senior boys and girls commenced their studies in the Secondary Modern School at Hasland Hall on

Hasland Junior School, Miss Pickard's class, 1954.
Back row: Miss Pickard, David Eyre, Howard Pickering, ?, David Makepeace, Eric Lowe,
Peter Walker, Ian Austin, Euan Moseley, Raymond Smith, Morgan Pickering.
3rd row: Margaret McDonald, Barbara Lowe, Nigel Smith, John Wier, Stuart Pickard, Howard Pitts,
Melvin Vaughan, Keith Parkes, Terrance Needham, Peter Haslam.
2nd row: Christine Baker, Ann Wilkinson, Margaret Shaw, Pamela Bagshaw, Pat Adnitt,
Susan Wilson, Valerie Dunn, Christine Lowe, Stephanie Pitchford, Rosalyn Wilbourne,
Jane Wheatcroft.
1st row: Margaret Hirst, Judith Halliday, Eileen Barlow, Janice Linney, Judith Coe, Joan Hopkinson,
Gillian Bestwick, Janet Parker, Reenee Vaines.

January 11th 1932. Mr B. C. Boden moved with the children from the headship of the Church of England School on The Green to be Headmaster of the new school. He was assisted by eight members of staff, these being Mr A. E. Pountain, Mr E. H. Simmons, Misses C. Beach, M. Heath, M. Stanley, P. Wildin, Mr O. J. Tonks and Miss Greenwood (part-time). Many years later, Mr Pountain recalled 'We were in the depression, teaching was secure, a job for life. As a result posts were hard to find. My first job was at Hasland Hall in Chesterfield, a mixed modern, and as my degree was in physics, I was engaged to teach biology and gardening. It was a large squirearchical sort of place with a big kitchen garden divided up into allotments and the boys did it all, growing lettuces, onions and fruit. We had thirty apple and thirty pear trees'. Apparently Mr Pountain was always very proud of his student's acheivements. Prior to the school opening major alterations had been carried out on the Hall resulting in large airy classrooms with much of the original beauty left.

The following is a report from the local press 'Hasland Modern Senior Mixed

Girl's sports team, Hasland Junior School, 1955.
Photograph courtesy of Joan Mullins.

Hasland Junior School football team, 1976

Hasland Junior School, 2004.

Hasland Hall Community School, 2004.

School which is to be opened on Monday is another monument to the enterprising and progressive spirit of the Chesterfield Education Committee. Hasland Hall, situated in ideal surrounds, has been admirably adapted to the purpose and great credit is due to the architects, Messrs.Wilcockson and Cutts, the contracter Mr C. Gaunt, and the clerk of works Mr T. J. Roberts, for the excellent manner in which the reconstruction and renovation have been carried out. Hasland Hall, for many years, was the residence of Mr Bernard Lucas J.P. and later of Mr Charles Markham J.P. The building has been converted into a thoroughly up-to-date modern school. From the large windows of all the classrooms a pleasant view is obtained of the wooded park. Such a beautiful environment will undoubtably prove an incentive to great efficiency, and as an excellent staff has been engaged it is anticipated that the building will quickly come to be recognised as one of the Town

Hasland Hall School teachers, c1935.
Mr Woolhouse, Mr Pountain, Mr Williams,
Mr Kelly.
Photograph courtesy of Joy Hungerford.

s leading elementary schools. There are two entrances to the school, one from Mansfield Road and the other from the Grassmoor Road. Ultimately there will be a third entrance in the vicinity of Storforth Lane. The cost of the Hall and site, including the lodge where the caretaker will reside was £4,500. The contract price amounted to £5,600. In view of the comments regarding subsidence it is interesting to note that during the restoration work, which has involved the temporary removal of many supports, there has been no sign of sinking. The staff will consist of eight trained certified teachers and each class will be limited to 40 scholars, and the practical work classes to 20. The school accommodates 288, and 280 scholars will be attending on Monday'.

The three Hasland schools, Eyre Street School, Hasland Junior School and Hasland Hall School are still open today.

Eyre Street School celebrated it's centenary last year (2004) when they held a week of activities, including dressing up in clothes from the period and taking part in lessons as they would have been 100 years ago. There was an exhibition of old photos and items of interest, and the children gave a concert entitled 'Songs from 100 Years'.

At the time of writing the main building of Hasland Junior School is due to be replaced by a new school which is to be built on the East side of Hasland Green.

Hasland Hall School. Boys gardening, c1935.
Photograph courtesy of Joy Hungerford.

Hasland Hall School. Boys at summer camp, c1935.
Photograph courtesy of Joy Hungerford.

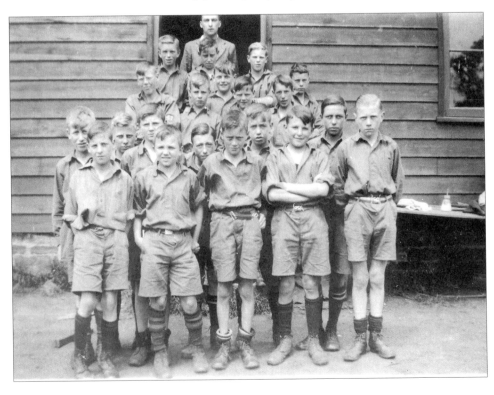

Hasland Hall School. Tug of war, c1935.
Photograph courtesy of Joy Hungerford.

Over the years Hasland Hall School, which is now known as Hasland Hall Community School, has undergone many alterations, the latest being a very large project which was started in 1992. This consisted of several new classrooms, six science laboratories, a sports hall with changing rooms and showers, a library, a reception foyer and two courtyards. It also included a new restaurant which was also to cater for the pupils of Hasland Junior School.

SCHOOL LOG BOOKS

Some excerpts from the log books of the Hasland Church Infant's School and Hasland Junior School.

Staff for 1899-1900
Miss H. E. Hollingworth – Certified teacher
Miss Fanny Lowe – Assist. under Art.50
May Handby – P.T. (Pupil Teacher) of the 4th year
Alice Ball – P.T. of the 1st year
Elizabeth Lowe – P.T. of the 1st year

Summary of H.M.Inspector's report 1899

The school is going on well the children being happy and interested and the instruction good.
Entered May 29th 1899 by William Barnes, manager and school correspondent.

June 30th

Ordinary school work. The Rev. W. Barnes visited the school on Monday morning and Friday afternoon. Very low attendance this week owing to much sickness among the children. A half holiday was given on Monday afternoon on account of the miner's demonstration.

Oct. 6th

Half holidays were given in the afternoons of Monday and Tuesday it being The Feast.

Nov. 3rd

A holiday was given on Wednesday on account of the visit from Barnum's show.

Feb.16th 1900

Very low average this week caused chiefly by bad weather. Obliged to close on Thursday and Friday, very few children and those assembled all had wet feet.

Feb.21st

School Inspection
Advisable to asphalt part of the playground.

Drawing sheets required.
K.G. table needs alteration.
Signed by W. T. Meggs.

List of Songs and Recitations for the year ending March 31st 1900

Merry Soldiers	The Red Fire
The Chickens	The London Train
The Truant	Learning to Grow
An Unpleasant Ride	The Hen s Complaint
Boys Wanted	The Boatblack

List of animal and object lessons to be given 1900-1901
The bat, dog, cat, seal, elephant, sheep, reindeer, camel, whale, hen, garoo, ostrich, frog, bee, tea, coffee, sugar, oak tree, gold, iron, salt, coal, slate, leather, bread, milk, water, setting the table, chair, table, clock face, good manners.

May 11th

A half holiday was given on Tuesday afternoon to prepare for a social for War Fund.

Summary of H.M. Inspector's Report 1900

The instruction continues to be given with great care and success the children are very orderly and attentive. The Infant School accommodation is at present insufficient for the average attendance. The attendance should be reduced or the accommodation increased.

May 25th

On Thursday a whole holiday was given on the occasion of the Queen's birthday.

July 13th

The attendances on Monday afternoon were cancelled owing to there being so few and the children were dismissed. There were two reasons for small attendance the Miner's Annual Demonstration and the Old People's Summer Treat.

Dec.14th

Many children absent this week owing to sickness, chiefly mumps.

Jan.14th 1901

Temperatures this morning at nine 43°

June 6th 1902

A holiday was given on Monday last on the occasion of the Proclamation of Peace.

June 24th

We break up this (Tuesday) afternoon for the rest of the week for Coronation holidays. Later: Since writing the above, news has arisen that Coronation is postponed therefore we must assemble tomorrow morning as usual all being well.

Feb. 6th 1903

Arrangements having been made for a holiday in anticipation of the King's visit to Chesterfield and Hardwick. It was given in spite of disappointment.

Sept. 4th

Re-opened school on Monday morning after month's holiday. School very overcrowded work difficult consequently.

Oct. 16th

A half-holiday was given on Friday afternoon owing to a visit from Wild West Show.

Oct. 23rd

The accommodation for the babies being most unsuitable under the best conditions, on wet days becomes intolerable and Mistress obliged to put two classes together and arrange lessons to suit both classes and their teachers.

Jan. 15th 1904
Visit of Inspection

This school is greatly over-crowded and many children have been refused permission. No children should be taught in the lobby. Today, 53 babies at one end of the cloak lobby, some even sitting on the lavatory. As it was a very wet morning the steam from the wet clothes made the plaster almost unbearable.

Apr. 8th

Re-opened school on Wednesday morning after Easter holiday. 36 boys were transferred to mixed school.

List of object lessons to be taken during the year 1904-1905 dog, bat, ostrich, owl, squirrel, kangaroo, whale, bee, giraffe, camel, cat, horse, cow, sheep, gold, leather, oak tree, buttercup, sugar, tea, coffee, chalk, slate, iron, salt, orange, apple, chair, table, setting the tea-table. The following have been selected from the above for the lowest class : horse, cow, sheep, cat, kangaroo, whale, dog, orange, apple, setting the tea-table, chair, table, tree, buttercup, sugar, gold.

H.M. Inspector's Report for 1902-1903

Infant School: Considering the over-crowding and the very difficult circumstances under which the school is working the instruction is very creditable. Needlework is markedly good. Very young children should not be admitted under the circumstances referred to above. This understood that temporary premises are now

engaged to give the necessary relief.
Signed C.S.W. Signed by William Barnes, School Correspondent. May 19th 1904.

Mar. 10th 1905

Ordinary school work on Monday morning. The names of 60 children were transferred to new Junior School. The remaining children were re-arranged and next year's work begun. Miss Mary Watson took the children to their new school and remained with them for the time being.

July 7th

This morning we received another visit from the Medical Officer of Health who examined all the children. This was on account of an outbreak of smallpox in the village.

July 14th

On Wednesday the school was closed at 11 in order that the teachers who wished to go to Sheffield on the occasion of their Majesty's visit might do so. Small attendance on account of smallpox scare.

July 21st

On Monday morning we received another visit from Medical Officer who examined all the children present, very low percentage, parents being afraid, in some cases, to send their children.

Mar. 23rd 1906

On Monday afternoon the school was closed in order that all might attend the funeral of our late Rector.

May 25th

A half-holiday was given on the afternoon of Thursday being Empire Day.

Feb. 8th 1907

Very low attendance owing to sickness. On Thursday morning there was no fire at all as a man was at work on the heating apparatus. Informed the Rector who came down and school was dismissed at 11.30 for the rest of the day.

Mar. 8th

School closed at 11a.m. by order of the Sanitary Authority owing to an epidemic of measles. The school to re-assemble on April 8th 1907 at 9a.m.
Horace H. Wilford

Mar. 8th

School closed this morning on account of measles epidemic. The Rev. H. H. Wilford brought in the order.

Apr. 12th

Re-opened school on Monday morning after month's closure. Many children still absent from sickness, chiefly whooping cough. 99 children were transferred to Junior School.

May 14th 1909

The temperature has been very low this week, below 50° most mornings at 9 o'clock.

June 11th

Re-opened school on Monday morning after week's holiday. Sent home a boy suffering from scabies.

Jan. 28th 1910

The weather this week has been very severe. Consequently the attendance has been very low. Today there was another flood in two rooms owing to melting snow. The children had to be crammed into the other two rooms which interferes with the teaching, and the aforesaid rooms are rendered very damp for days after, which is prejudicial to the health of both children and teachers.

May 27th

Re-opened school after Whitsuntide holiday. Very many cases of whooping cough and a few cases of scarlet fever.

Nov. 9th

Today we have become part of the Borough of Chesterfield.

Feb. 3rd 1911

On Tuesday Miss F. Lowe, assistant, severed her connection with this school after faithful and diligent service of many years.

May 1st

Copy of H.M.I.Report
Infants
In many respects this is a good infant's school. It has been much improved by the headmistress in the last few years. The two comparatively small sections of the upper class have made good progress during the year. The children in the upper section are very bright and intelligent. The teachers of the other two classes are doing their best, but one has 70 children and the other 87. With so many children it is of course impossible for them to provide suitable training,
Horace H.Wilford.

June 16th

School assembled on Monday after Whitsuntide holiday. We beak up this (Friday) afternoon for Coronation holiday of one week.

Oct. 4th

Mistress given a holiday until Wednesday morning in order to take the baths at Matlock for rheumatism. On Wednesday morning there was no fire and the thermometer stood at 41°. On the previous morning it read 46°.

May 24th 1912

Empire Day – Talks about our King and Country and singing patriotic songs and saluting the flag took place from 11 to 11.45. We broke up for Whitsuntide holidays and many cases of sickness.

Apr. 1st 1913

Report of Religious Knowledge Exam
The work throughout has been exceedingly well nicely done and the children showed themselves most happy and interested and answered with thorough understanding of what they had learnt and with delightful naturalness.
W. Vivian Davis, April 1st 1913

May 19th

Re-opened school after Whitsun holiday. Only 50% of the children in attendance owing to the great increase in measles cases.

May 23rd

School closed for a fortnight by order of Dr. Sharpe, Schools Medical Officer.

July 4th

On Wednesday a holiday was given in order that the children might participate in the festivities attending the opening of the Eastwood Park.

Oct. 14th

Re-opened school after 10 week's closure caused by alterations to mixed school which made the yard unsafe for children. As will be acknowledged what has to be considered is not only what the children have not learnt but what they have forgotten. On the other hand many of them have benefited in health by the prolonged holiday as the school has had a sickly time from the beginning of the year.

Dec. 18th

Received a consignment of oranges from the Mayor (Ald. E. Shentall J.P.) to be given to children.

Mar. 6th 1914

Ordinary school work. Many admissions recently. Every class filled to it 's utmost capacity.

Apr. 8th

We break up this (Wednesday) afternoon for Easter holiday. 3 cases of diphtheria.

May 22nd

Nearly 30 known cases of whooping cough this week. Attendance very low.

Oct. 15th 1915

This school is to be closed from today noon until the morning of Wednesday next week, in order that the teachers may help with registration (National) work.

Feb. 25th 1916

Very low attendance – 84 this morning owing to a heavy snowstorm.

Jan. 12th 1917

Reopened school on Monday after Christmas holidays – on the worst days I ever remember, consequently the attendance was very low. Bad weather continued all the week. On certain days the children were allowed to leave as early as possible – 3.30 – in order to obviate the necessity of sitting any longer with wet feet.

Feb. 23rd

Have reported 10 known cases of chicken pox to M.O.H. (schools)

Apr. 11th

Reopened school on Wednesday morning in bitterly cold weather. Thermometer stood at 33° at 9 o'clock. Very poor attendance.

Sept. 28th

Very satisfactory attendance for the month – the best in this school's record.

Nov. 7th 1918

Closed school today (Thursday) on account of prevalence of influenza. Eventually the school remained closed for 8 weeks.

May 30th 1919

Miss Annie Watson terminates her work in this school after 9 years of devoted service. More cases of fever.

July 4th

A holiday was given on Wednesday to commemorate the Signing of Peace.

July 25th

A holiday was given on Monday and Tuesday for Peace Celebrations.

Oct. 3rd

School work as usual. We break up today for the 'King's' holiday of 1 week.

Feb. 20th 1920

This (Friday) morning there was a deep snow consequently there was a very poor attendance, only 62 being present out of a roll of 206.

June 11th

Reported 37 cases of whooping cough today. Low attendance.

Oct. 29th

Mistress handed in her notice of resignation this morning after 42 year's service in this school as Mistress.

Dec. 10th

Low attendance this week, caused by sickness, 5 cases of diphtheria. Also towards the end of the week, by children absenting themselves after a visit to the clinic to have teeth extracted.

Dec. 23rd

Mistress leaves today.

Jan. 10th 1921

Re-opened school after Xmas holidays – 2 weeks. This department reorganised.
Staff
Bert C. Bowden
E. B. Roe
A. Martin
O. W. Ingle
D. Robinson
G. Bower
M. Allibone
A. Lignum

Admitted 166 children from Eyre St. Working a free time table this week & until organisation is more settled.

Mar. 15th

A class of boys attended a lecture on Coal Mining.

June 3rd

The school work was further interrupted by necessary reorganisation in connection with the feeding of necessitous children.

July 8th

It has been intensely hot this week.

July 25th

The Master left school at 3 to attend the unveiling of a War Memorial at Doveridge where he was formerly headmaster.

Sept. 1st

Arranged with Miss Mason for an urgent requisition. Stand 2. Class H having a very inadequate supply of books.

Sept. 22nd

This p.m. the top class visited Wingerworth. The Rev.W.R.Coleman, Rector, gave the children a most interesting talk on the church – architectural & other features.

Nov. 11th

Half holiday this afternoon as recognition of Armistice Day.

Feb. 28th 1922

Shrove Tuesday, and occasion of the marriage of H.R.H. Princess Mary. At the request of H.M. The King, the Committee granted a whole holiday.

May 3rd

The very inclement weather having interfered with gardening operations, a special effort was made today & sowings of parsnips, kohl rabi, beet, peas & potatoes made.

May 15th

Circular no.5 issued from Ed.Office gives instructions; that the Town Council have decided to introduce into Chesterfield the rule of the road Keep to the left for pedestrians, and children are to be taught accordingly.

Oct. 5th

At the request of the secretary, sent in estimate of expenditure for forthcoming six months as under

Books & Stationary	400 @ 2/6	£50
Needlework Materials	Nett cost	£4
Furniture & Repairs		£20
Light	as last year	?
Fuel	48 loads of coke	

> 2 loads of coal   ?
> 200 bundles of wood

Apr. 26th 1923

Today – the occasion of the marriage of H.R.H. The Duke of York with Lady Elizabeth Bowes-Lyon, the school is granted a whole holiday at the request of H.M. The King.

May 24th

This day being Empire Day the usual morning lessons were devoted to suitable 'lessons on Empire'. The Master provided a gramophone record of a speech to children by H.M. The King and a message by H.M. The Queen. The afternoon session is a recognised holiday.

Sept. 17th

Received information from the secretary that there will be a half holiday on Thursday afternoon in connection with the Shopping Festival.

Oct. 18th

The Medical Officer intimated that the Public Vaccinator would attend for the purpose of vaccinating children whose parents agreed. Dr. Robinson & Fraser were present this morning from 10.30 a.m. and vaccinated seventy-nine children. The attendance in the afternoon was low.

Jan. 26th 1925

Mr Mason (stores clerk) called. He informed the Master that the half yearly requisition could not be allowed, as 'funds were exhausted'. (This happened last year).

May 4th

Mr Mason, stores clerk, called with regard to the requisitions sent last Feby. It appears that the goods have not yet been ordered. There is not an exercise book in school.

May 21st

This day being Ascension Day, the children were taken to church in accordance with ancient custom. Mr A. E. Heath M.A. formerly scholar in this school was on Monday (18th) elected to the Chair of Philosophy, University of Wales.

June 24th

Award of Minor Scholarships.
The proportion of scholarships awarded to this school out of those allocated to the Chesterfield Borough Attendance

District is 7/43 – George Boam, Topsy Buddle, Pearl Fisher, Dennis Knight, Gertrude Naylor, Thomas Sharpe, Horace Smith.

Nov. 27th

Today the funeral service of the late Queen Alexandra takes place in Westminster Abbey. By permission of the secretary the T.T. was adjusted so that the children might attend a Memorial Service at Hasland Church.

May 20th 1926

A party of children from the top classes – headmaster in charge, visited B.T.H. Works at Chesterfield.

July 14th 1927

See Apr. 8th (Stationary Requisition)

Arndis account £10/7/1, also a/c for pen nibs 15/- checked & signed. Mr Brown's a/c for repairing of a teacher s desk and sewing cupboard is 6/5. In addition to these repairs the broken panes of glass were replaced last week. The door has been off the sewing cupboard for eighteen months & some of the panes broken since last October!

Oct. 12th

The Master left school this p.m. at 2.30 in order to attend the opening ceremony at the Technical College.

Apr. 26th 1928

By permission of the director the children were photographed this afternoon, the first time for 12 years.

May 7th

Received intimation that the Chief Constable will address the school on Friday May 18th at 2.30 on Safety First .

July 6th

Received notification that a visit to Markham Works has been arranged for a party of 16 boys on July 24th.

Sept. 26th

The Master left school this p.m. to attend the opening of the Violet Markham School for girls. A general invitation & permission having been issued from the office to all head teachers.

Sept. 27th 1928

Very handsome prizes – engraved boxes of drawing instruments arrived for H.

Metcalf & G. Pell, winners of Messrs. Markham & Co essay prizes (see entry on July 6th) I wish to place on record an appreciation of the unstinted generosity & of the hospitality shown by Messrs. Markham to the class who visited the works on the arranged date.

May 16th 1930

The supply of milk (1/3pt for 1d) at 10.40 has been in operation for the past two weeks & is satisfactory.

July 9th

Twenty boys visited Messrs. Bryan Donkin & Co. Engineering Works – Mr Simmons in charge.

July 16th

The Master left at 3 to attend the opening of the new R.C. School, general permission from office.

Nov. 11th

Armistice Day celebrations – sale of poppies (Earl Haig Fund) conducted as instructed by the director.

Mar. 16th 1931

The amount of allowances for the forthcoming year is as under

Apparatus	Domestic Subjects	Handicraft
£70/10/9	£27/0/0	£50/8/4

Dec. 23rd

Closed school for Xmas holidays.
The Headmaster with the following members of the staff – E. H. Simmons, E. A. Pountain, M. Heath, P. M. Wildin, M. Stanley, C. Beach are leaving for the new Senior School at Hasland Hall, the Headmaster thus completing 24 years service under the management of the School Managers
Bert C. Bowden 23/12/31

Jan. 11th 1932

The school was opened after the Christmas vacation as the Hasland Junior Mixed School.
Staff
Mr H. Keeton   Head Master
Mr F. Cooper
Miss D. Pickard
Miss G. Powell
Miss D. Beach

Miss M. M. Wadsworth

July 7th
The Head Teacher left at 2.50 to attend the official opening of the Hasland Hall School.

July 8th
The percentage of attendance for the week is 93.6. The school was closed at 3.45 p.m. to allow the staff & children to attend a tea in Eastwood Park, given by Miss Eastwood.

July 4th 1933
On the occasion of Their Majesties the King & Queen passing through Hasland the children were paraded on the Green at 2.50p.m. After Their Majesties had passed the children were marched back to school & dismissed.

Nov. 29th 1934
The school was closed today in accordance with the wish expressed by His Majesty the King, today being the wedding day of His Royal Highness the Duke of Kent.

May 6th 1935
The school was closed on the occasion of the Jubilee of H.M.King George 5th.

Nov. 6th
The school was closed today on the occasion of the marriage of H.R.H. The Duke of Gloucester.

Jan. 28th 1936
A short memorial to His Late Majesty was taken followed by special lessons on the main events of the Late King's Reign and the experiences of His Majesty King Edward 8th. The school was closed at 11.30 a.m.

Feb. 28th
The Headmaster left at 3.45 p.m. to attend the opening of the New Children's Library.

Oct. 28th
The school was opened after the October break. Reported that a scholar in the school, age 8, had died from diphtheria.

Nov. 4th
The S.M.O. & the Assist. S.M.O. visited the school this morning & immunised 99 children against diphtheria.

May 11th 1937

The school was closed at 4 p.m. today for the Coronation Festivities & the Whitsun holidays.

July 27th

The top class accompanied by the Head Teacher & Mr Cooper visited the Hasland Loco Sheds this afternoon.

Jan. 24th 1938

Work was commenced on the turfing of the spare ground in front of the school & on the South Side.

Apr. 6th

The school was closed this afternoon on the occasion of the opening of the New Town Hall. Mary Norman & Eric Barlow represented the school at the opening.

Mar. 8th 1939

The school was closed at 3.30 p.m. to enable the staff to attend a meeting in the Market Hall – Evacuation of children during war.

Apr. 27th

The Head Teacher left at 2 p.m. to attend the opening of Brambling House School.

Aug. 29th

Gas masks were brought to school – fitted & labelled.

Sept. 11th 1939

The school was closed until further notice owing to War being declared.

Sept. 13th 1940

103 children absent this morning – air raid during night. The percentage of attendance for the week is 86.1.

Sept. 24th

A terrible tragedy occurred this morning. The Headmaster, Mr Keeton, collapsed and died almost immediately. Dr Allison had been called in and was present at the time. Dr Stead ordered school to be closed for the afternoon.

Nov. 1st

I – (Herbert Bavin) commenced duty as Headmaster. The percentage of attendance for the week is 81.2 – measles epidemic.

Dec. 17th

Afternoon school interrupted by an alert from 2.5 p.m to 4.5 p.m. Classes 1, 2, 3 and 4 were accommodated in the Senior School shelter & classes 5, 6 and 7 in the cellar.

Feb. 13th 1942

The school Savings Group raised £441 this week in investment in the Local Warship Week effort.

June 11th

The school staged a sports programme this afternoon. This was a first venture. The school had been divided into four teams – preliminary heats were run off & a programme prepared. The afternoon proved successful. Mr Fowler H.M.I. was present.

Sept. 9th

Received results of recent waste paper collection. The school collected over 12lb per head & received the 2nd peace award of £2/0/0. Beryl Hardstaff received 10/- prize for 1st place in the Junior Schools Handwriting Compn.

Jan. 19th 1943

The school meals service was today available for children from this school – 84 meals were served at mid-day to children from the school, who dined in the hall of the Hasland Hall School.

Apr. 12th – 17th

The School National Savings Group participated in the Chesterfield Wings for Victory week. A total of £780 was invested through the group during the week. A further £8 7s 6d was sent as a gift as a result of various efforts .

Oct. 4th

Milk again supplied in 1/3 pint bottles (& straws). Demand increased from 11 galls. per day to (approx.) 16½ galls. per day.

Apr. 26th 1944

This week being special Salute the Soldier savings effort – the school group fixed a target of £750 – the result was a total of £1,500 invested during the week.

July 20th

A goodly number of evacuees from London and the Southern Counties have been admitted this week (32).

Aug. 28th

The school reopened after the holiday. The school has 376 children on books – (includes 58 evacuees). There is a considerable shortage of seating – wrote asking for additional desks.

Aug. 29th

Miss Spooner (L.C.C.) joined the staff – Miss Spooner is an evacuee teacher from L.C.C. Formed an additional class, from 2nd year to work with Miss Spooner in the staff room.

Oct. 13th

Following instruction from the C.E.O., removed all seating and other equipment from the school air-raid shelter, which is now 1 foot deep in water.

Mar. 29th 1945

The school closed at mid-day for the normal Easter holiday. The Head Teacher completed duty here – having been transferred to Old Road Junior & Infant's School as from 1st April 45.

Apr. 9th

I – Doris A.Taylor commenced duty as temporary Headmistress.

May 8th

Declared a public holiday for victory in Europe. Schools closed Tuesday and Wednesday.

July 13th

Reduced attendance due to local collieries holidays.

Feb. 28th 1946

I, Doris A.Taylor, cease duties here, as temporary head-teacher, today. Transfer to The Brushes Primary School to replace the retiring head-teacher Mrs Rollinson.

Mar. 1st

I (Arthur W.Greaves) commenced duty today as Headmaster.

May 30th

A Mr Allison visited the school this morning. He is a trainee under the Government Scheme for training of teachers from men in the Forces. He will be attached to the staff of this school from Monday next.

Feb. 4th 1947

An abnormal snowfall due to a blizzard last night has caused almost half the school to be away this morning, 184 children are present out of 353 (52%). All the staff managed to get here though most were late owing to difficulties of transport. Certain roads in the district are absolutely impassable.

Feb. 13th

The school closed at 4 p.m. for the half term holiday (Friday & Monday). In addition two extra days will be taken throughout the Borough on account of lack of fuel stocks for heating school premises.

Feb. 20th

The school reopened this morning. Full staff present. Attendance slightly better. During the holiday Mr Ernest Randall, the Caretaker, died suddenly. Temporary help has been sent.

Feb. 21st

Miss Cox, Miss Stubbs and Mrs Plews of the staff of Eyre Street Primary Infants reported for duty at this school this morning. The Eyre Street School is closed for four extra days on account of the cold and the fuel shortage.

Apr. 28th

Mr Wilfred Dumelow commenced duties as School Caretaker this day.

July 24th

One hundred and twenty children are away from school today. The majority of these have gone on an outing to Cleethorpes arranged by the Working Men's Club in Hasland.

Nov. 19th

The school closed at 4 p.m. today for one day's holiday on the occasion of the wedding tomorrow of Princess Elizabeth.

Jan. 14th 1948

School reopened this morning after the Christmas holiday. Full staff present. For the first time the Headmaster had to refuse admission to two children owing to classes in two age groups being full.

Jan. 19th

Staff at Commencement of Year

Mr A. W. Greaves	Headmaster	
Miss D. M. Pickard	Deputy Head	Class 1
Mr J. Esland		Class 2
Miss W. Jephson		Class 3
Miss F. Haynes		Class 4

Mrs M. Langenus	Class 5
Miss K. H. Pearson	Class 6
Miss M. Dobb	Class 7
Miss J. Mullins	Class 8
Mr R. G. Morris	
Mr F. P. Tiramani	

Apr. 26th

The upper school assembled in rooms 1 & 3 to listen to the Radio Broadcast on the occasion of Their Majesty's Silver Wedding Anniversary. The school closed at 12 noon for the holiday granted by the King. Today school dinners commenced in the Temperance Hall, Eyre Street, in our own temporary dining hall.

June 23rd

In the afternoon, Mr C. Yates, architect, came up to inspect the condition of the roof, which owing to subsidence has caused water to pour into classes 1 & 2 & the two cloakrooms after heavy rain. He was accompanied by an asphalt roofing expert and they decided to re rock-asphalt certain parts of the roof.

Sept. 9th

Mr A. Greenough, Borough Education Officer, visited the school and discussed my ideas for removing part of lawn, extending the playground and making good paths at the front of the school. In this way both entrances can be used to get children into school and the overcrowding and danger in the playground would be lessened.

Mar. 22nd 1949

Today's Sheffield Telegraph reported on last night's Education Committee Meeting which gave notice of the proposed addition to this school of two classrooms. This a.m. Mr C. Tates, deputy architect, visited the school to make arrangements for the asphalting of the proposed extension to the playground.

Mar. 24th

This afternoon two police officers tested the cycles of twenty children and made reports on their condition.

Jan. 9th 1950

School reopened this a.m. full staff present. Today the new dining hall was used for the first time.

Mar. 3rd

The attendance this week has been the lowest since I came to the school (76.75%). Nearly one quarter of the school is absent owing to flu epidemic, jaundice, etc.

Oct. 30th

School reopened today after the mid-term break. Full staff present. During the holiday the Adult School, in Storforth Lane, which has been requisitioned by the Ministry, was inspected with a view to renting by the Authority. It is a well built Hall and would be a great asset to this school in order.

Dec. 19th

The School Party was held today in the School Dining Hall. 370 children sat down together at 2.30 p.m. and were waited on by the staff and friends who had previously prepared the tables, food, etc. After the eating was over the children were entertained by a dancing display given by the pupils of Miss B. Blakesley, by a Royal Punch and Judy Show given by Mr S. Brunning and finally by Mr W. Lawrence illusionist.

Jan. 8th 1951

School reopened this a.m. Full staff present. During the holiday the Hasland Adult School has been acquired by the Authority and orders put out to put it into a fit state for use. Electricity, gas, fittings, heating system, need checking and putting in order, and some repairs to the roof will be necessary. It is hoped to have this hall ready within a few weeks.

Feb. 15th 1952

There was no morning service held this a.m. A special service was arranged for the funeral of His Late Majesty King George 6th. Two minutes silence was observed at 2p.m. (as nationally). Special prayers in form prescribed for use in schools were read and a talk on the life of the late King, and the new Queen was given to the children. Two of the late King's favourite hymns ('Abide With Me' and 'The King of Love my Shepherd is') were sung and the service was concluded by the singing of the National Anthem. The school closed at 3.50 for the mid term holiday.

Dec. 8th

The Borough Education Officer, Mr A. Greenough called this morning to discuss accommodation now the new block is completed. The Head pointed out the growing urgency for a new school as the new annexe would only ease the position for this year. A further three stream year is expected to be admitted next September in addition to the numbers due from a new estate of 100 houses in Calow Lane & Spital Lane. Further extensive building plans by the National Coal Board are likely to bring in a possible extra 200 children in the next few years and provision will have to be made for these. The B.E.O. said that the site for a new Junior School was earmarked and that the whole matter would be raised in Committee in the near future.

June 1st. 1953

The school is still closed for the three days special Coronation Holiday. Several of the male staff came to school to complete decorations in rooms and outside the school.

June 2nd

Coronation Day.

June 3rd

Full staff assembled at 9a.m. to prepare for the Coronation celebrations. Owing to the rain and the intense cold it was decided to postpone the actual sports until a more favourable date. Children assembled at 2p.m. and an impromptu concert was held until the time the tea was ready. The Coronation tea was held in the two Dining Halls and the fourth year were accommodated in the new annexe. Councillor S. Bell presented the Souvenir Book 'Elizabeth Our Queen' to all children present and Messrs. W. Heathcote and W. Halliday (representing the Parent's Committee) presented souvenir brooches & tie pins to all children.

Nov. 17th

The whole of the 3rd and 4th years with 8 staff visited the Regal Cinema to see the film 'Conquest of Everest' at 2p.m. this afternoon.

Jan. 15th 1954

Heard today that the Caretaker has applied to the Authority for permission to vacate the school house in order to live in his own home which has become vacant. I have made application to the Borough Educ. Officer for the house premises to be added to the school to provide Staff Rooms & lavatory accommodation, and a medical inspection room, which are so urgently required. The fourth room could be used as a special reading, or domestic room and could house the School Library.

Apr. 9th

The school closes today for the Easter vacation. Mr Dumelow today ceased his duties as Caretaker.

Apr. 26th

School reopened after the Easter holiday. Mr Boot commenced his duties as Caretaker. Full staff present.

Dec. 14th

A party of 22 children left school at 9.20 a.m. to attend the Regal Cinema for the Sheffield Telegraph Toy Distribution Scheme for poor children at Christmas. Mr H.Morgan accompanied the party which returned to school after a film show at 11.30 a.m.

Sept. 27th 1955

The Borough Education Officer visited to inform me that according to the County Surveyor, new workings on the Piper Seam from Grassmoor Colliery are due to pass under the school in 1956-7 and that damage from subsidence is likely to school property.

Feb. 9th 1956

The Headmaster left school at 10.15 a.m. to attend the funeral of Sir George Kenning.

Sept. 12th

P.C. Goodall, Road Safety, arranged the demonstration of Road Safety in the playground with the Upper School. A street complete with signs, zebra crossing, beacons, studs & vehicles was set up. The Borough Education Officer visited during the demonstration.

Mar. 1st 1957

The Headmaster was absent from school in the afternoon on the occasion of the visit of the Hon.Hugh Gaitskill, Leader of the Opposition, to Bradbury Hall on the occasion of Tapton House Speech Day which he attended.

Feb. 13th 1958

A representative of the firm of Bowater visited school this morning to discuss the provision of paper towels & containers for this school which is one selected by the Authority to try out the scheme for two years.

Feb. 25th

A particularly heavy snowfall all night. Transport difficult. Only three teachers present by 9a.m. to open school. Others came in at intervals. Only Miss Martin failed to turn in. She has a severe cold. 165 children absent today – mainly the younger ones. Commenced afternoon session at 1p.m. and cut out break – letting the children go home at 3p.m.

Feb. 27th

The Transfer Exam scheduled for today throughout the County has been cancelled on account of the heavy snow conditions.

May 2nd

The Head Teacher left school at 2.45 p.m. to visit the Edwin Swale School for the official opening by Sir John Wolfenden, Vice Chancellor of Reading University.

Nov. 21st

100 children from the upper school, selected by lot, met at school at 2.15p.m. where,

accompanied by the Headmaster, Messrs. Esland, Roberts, Morris, Owen & Mesdames Langenus and Atkinson they embarked in buses and were conducted to a reserved enclosure in front of the Town Hall for the Prince s visit. The children returned to school after the ceremony for dismissal.

Dec. 9th

The Architect Mr Chas.Yates accompanied by three officials of the N.C.B. inspected the school building inside and out. As mining is to come almost underneath the school they decided on certain preventative methods to deal with any subsidence. Outside it was decided to cut a four inch channel round the building and to fill this with sand. On the inside all the high plaster ceilings were thought to be in danger of cracking and to prevent any fall these were to be covered with board.

May 6th 1960

School closed on the occasion of the Royal Wedding of Princess Margaret to Mr Armstrong Jones.

July 15th

The children in the first year, today had a coach tour of Derbyshire visiting the new Ogston Reservoir, Crich Stand, Matlock & Chatsworth.

July 19th 1961

School closes today at 4p.m. on the occasion of the All England Athletic Championship to be held at Chesterfield this weekend.

Jan. 11th 1963

The temperature this week has been the lowest on record -7°F (-18°C) in the day time. The gas heaters in the Annex have proved totally inadequate – the floor temperature in the rooms being below 40°F. Classes have been doubled up with the rooms with electric heaters. In spite of the severe conditions attendance for the week was 94%.

Feb. 28th

Mr Harold Webb, the Chesterfield Road Safety Officer, visited to discuss the use of the playground for Cycle Proficiency Tests.

Mar. 1st

Today marks the end of the eleventh week of arctic weather with below zero temperatures. The school playground is still covered with deep frozen snow from Christmas time. Attendance remarkably good.

May 3rd

The school was closed today on the occasion of the Royal Visit of Princess Margaret and Earl Snowden to Chesterfield. Ninety children were taken by bus to the school children's enclosure in front of the Town Hall.

July 26th

This afternoon presentations were made to Mrs Jackson who leaves the staff for domestic reasons and to Mr Nicholson who is transferring to Rother School. Together with Miss Pickard they terminate their service at this school today.

Miss Pickard has been Deputy Head at this school since it was structurally altered and converted into a Junior School in 1932. For thirty one years she has given wonderful service here under three Headmasters and a temporary Headmistress. In all she has completed 37 years service in the Borough.

Sept. 11th

Mr Matthews, Deputy Education Officer, visited at lunch time to inform me that the annex at the Adult School was to be sold and that we should shortly – in mid October – be terminating our tenancy of the building. I undertook to furnish a list of what furniture & apparatus we should need at school and which would need taking away to be put into store.

Jan.14th 1964

During the morning the School Architect visited together with a Mr Fox of the National Coal Board who informed me that a second seam of coal lying beneath the school is now to be worked out. This will mean subsidence again on a possibly larger scale than before. The N.C.B. is to inspect the building to decide on certain safety precautions which need to be taken. It is just over five years ago since the first Piper seam of coal was scheduled to be worked & we were notified accordingly.

Feb. 11th 1965

Mr J. Esland visited Hasland Infant s School to see the working of the I.T.A. scheme with very young children.

Sept. 13th

The new timetable was put into operation this morning. French is now a full part of the school curriculum beginning in the second year – throughout both streams of the third and fourth years.

Sept. 21st

Mr Taylor, the Borough Education Officer, visited the school this morning – a personal call on account of my letter of resignation as Head Teacher of this school pending my retirement at Christmas.

Jan. 10th 1966

Mr Frederick Cyril Keeton commenced duties as Headmaster (Appointment w/e

1.1.66).

July 20th

Parents of first & second year children attended a meeting at which headmaster outlined his plans for re-organising school under system of non-streaming.

Sept. 6th 1967

The Headmaster attended the official opening of the new Youth Centre which the children are allowed to use during the daytime for Assembly, P.E. & Movement.

Sept. 9th

School re-opened today with full staff present. The two terrapin classrooms handed over to us although the interior fittings are not complete.

Oct. 19th

The headmaster went to the official opening of the new Chesterfield School.

Dec. 6th 1982

This is to record formally the death of the headmaster Mr F.C.Keeton after a month's illness due to a fall at home. Mr Keeton died at 2pm on Saturday 4th December in the Royal Hospital. All school will miss Mr Keeton more than words can express, since for so many years he was the school, in every sense, as well as being guide and friend to us all.

May 16th 1983

Mr Gilby, new head teacher, spent the day in school meeting staff and discussing arrangements for next educ. year.

SNIPPETS FROM THE NEWSPAPERS

The Derbyshire Times Saturday January 19th 1907

A well-known man in Hasland passed away on Friday in Mr Joseph Severn a driver on the Midland Railway. He was for many years a member of the committee of the Hasland Flower Show and when it was started for the second time he was the Chairman until it's dissolution last year. At the funeral on Tuesday the coffin was borne by his workmates from the Hasland Engine Sheds.

The Derbyshire Times Saturday 3rd December 1910

It was decided at a special meeting of the Hasland Parish Council on Tuesday to let the contract for health scavenging from December to March 31st 1911 to Mr W.White, Grassmoor and if a second horse and cart was required to ask Mr W. Gilding to do the work. The fire brigade to Grassmoor will now consist of the Messrs. T. Atkin(captain), J. Rush, J. Smith and J. King in the place of Sergeant Moorcroft resigned. The two members for The Green will be Mr W. Heathcote and Mr W. Gelsthorpe and the two for Winsick, Messrs Mr E. Oldham and H. Hall. Mr J. A. Oxley presided at the meeting and the others present were Messrs J. Whitworth, A. J. Cole, T. Whitworth, W. Sexton and W. Hollingworth (clerk).

The Derbyshire Times Saturday January 18th 1913

Hasland people are indignant at the attempt being made to wreck the Chesterfield Trackless Tramway Bill. The poll is fixed for Monday week. All those who wish to see a Tramway extension to Hasland should not fail to vote on that day for the Corporation's Bill.

The Derbyshire Times Saturday 31st May 1913

A good many of the scholars attending the Infant School, Hasland were very much elated when they were told they could have a fortnights holiday from last Friday afternoon. There is a mild epidemic of measles in the village about 40 children being affected and an order was given to close the schools for two weeks to prevent as far as possible the disease spreading.

The Derbyshire Times Saturday January 25th 1913

Please note, a Grand Bazaar will be held in the new Temperance Hall, Hasland on Tuesday and Wednesday the 28th and 29th inst. opened each day at 2p.m. Everybody heartily invited. Admission 6d each. Tickets can be obtained from F. Witham, Handby Street, Hasland, Secretary, G. Hopkinson, Mansfield Road, Treasurer or any member of The Order. (Advt)

The Derbyshire Times Saturday 5th December 1914

Since the War broke out a rifle range has been acquired at the Hasland Workingmen's Club and to encourage proficiency in shooting a tournament was soon arranged. There were three finalists with a score of 47 out of a possible 50. These shot off on Saturday and Mr F. Jacobs proved the winner by scoring 48. Mr T. Reeves followed next with 45 and then came Mr Naylor with 44.

The Derbyshire Times Saturday 5th December 1914

Wednesday and Thursday nights were red-letter ones for the children of Eyre Street Council School, Hasland as they gave two concerts in the Village Hall, Eastwood Park in aid of the Prince of Wales and Belgian Relief Funds. The stage in the hall had been enlarged free of cost by Mr F. Beardow. The children had been trained by the headmistress Miss J. F. Hardy assisted by Mrs A. Wadsworth, Misses C. Ball, A. Cooper B. Ashcroft, H. Askey and A. Jones. The accompanists were the Misses Ashcroft and Ball, Mrs Wadsworth and Mr T. Moseley. Miss Eastwood presided the first night and Alderman E. Shentall the second. The programme opened with the singing of the English National Anthem by Miss B. Ashcroft and the choir. Then came 'La Brabanconne', the Belgian National Anthem and of course the Russian and French Anthems followed. Elgar's 'Land of Hope and Glory' by Miss Ashcroft and the choir preceded an interesting Union Jack flag drill given by eighteen of the girls and choir. The second part of the programme was taken up with something quite new to Hasland audiences and was much appreciated. It consisted of songs and dances of olden days. There were Christmas, Holly, Mistletoe, Frost and Snow, Morris, Rose, Old English Country, Handkerchief and Stick dances. These were interspersed with some fine old English folk songs. A Fairy Operetta opened the third and last part of the entertainment. This was 'Little Bo-peep', the title character being taken by Lucy Scott. Ida Wheatcroft was the Snowdrop Queen of the Fairies. Gertie Austin 'Mischief', Edna Humberstone 'Buttercup', and Lizzie Wheatcroft 'Daisy'.

The Derbyshire Courier March 27th 1915

At the opening of the Victoria Billiard Hall, Hasland on Wednesday, an exhibition game was played between F. W. Hughes, the ex-Yorkshire champion (Leeds), and young Joe Davis the Derbyshire boy champion. Hughes conceded his young opponent 200 in a game of 600 up. In the early stages of the game the ex-champion gained ground gradually with breaks of 24, 27, 33, 21 and 65. The boy cuist made compilations of 21, 27, 23, 20 and 41, while he crowned his efforts by running to points with a splendid 99 unfinished. Final score, Davis 600, Hughes 370.

The Derbyshire Courier Saturday April 10th 1915

In celebration of the anniversary of the opening of the Primitive Methodist Church, Hasland special services were held on Good Friday. In the afternoon Mr Barnet Kenyon M.P. preached at a well attended service. Tea was provided to which over 100 sat down. The arrangements being carried out the by lady members of the Church. A public meeting in the evening was presided over by Mr J. W. Lee, speakers being Mr Barnet Kenyon, the Rev. J. Pickett and the Rev. W. Vaughan. A special visit was paid to the Church on Sunday by the Rev J. W. Musson, Kiveton Park, who is to succeed the Rev. W. Vaughan in July. The prospective minister preached both morning and evening and also addressed the Bible Class in the afternoon. Mrs Allsop was very pleasing as soloist.

The Derbyshire Courier Tuesday April 6th 1915
Y.M.C.A. FOR SOLDIERS HASLAND BRANCH

The opening night of the above on Monday last was a great success and a convincing argument (if one was needed) of the usefulness of such a branch for the soldiers of Hasland Hall. The premises have been placed at the disposal of the Committee free so the expenses will not be great. At this time of many appeals we venture to ask for the subscriptions. We shall be pleased of course to receive them from any source but address our appeal especially to the residents of Hasland in the confident hope that they will consider it a privilege to help to minister to the comfort and add to the pleasures of the men of the Army Service Corps in their midst. Subscription will be gladly received by any member of the local Committee or by the Honourable Treasurer, Mr Jno. W. Lee, Belmont Hasland Chesterfield. On behalf of the Committee the Rev. Vivian Davies, Chairman, C. P. Norman, Hon. Secretary, March 30th 1915

The Derbyshire Courier Tuesday April 6th 1915

Soldiers numbering upwards of 200 together with Major Buller and other officers quartered with the Army Service Corps at Hasland Hall were entertained to a highly enjoyable evening on Monday under the auspices of the Young Men's Christian Association. The event signalled the opening of rooms in the Wesleyan School which have been placed at the disposal of the Association for the recreation of the entertainment of soldiers and it was a marked success. The Rector of Hasland the Rev. W. V. Davies occupied the chair. A programme of miscellaneous items was well rendered the soldiers showing their appreciation in marked style. Songs were sung by Misses M. Hallam, I. Barlow, Messrs. H. Unwin, C, Barlow, Jacob and H. B. Saxton. While one of the guests Driver Leach also contributed to the programme. Acting as accompanist was Mr Paul Wheatcroft. Refreshments were served at intervals by members of the local Committee of which Mr C. P. Norman is secretary.

The Derbyshire Courier May 8th 1915

Mr T. H. Moseley has resigned his position as Bandmaster to the Hasland Silver Prize Band after many years of excellent service. As a miner, Mr Moseley worked at the no.3 pit of the Grassmoor Colliery Company but he has now obtained employment at the Mansfield Colliery where he joins his two sons Harry and Arthur. The former of whom was also connected with the band as a cornet player. Mr Moseley who also, in addition as tutor, was a player of the pianoforte and was ready to lend his services as accompanist to any discerning object and there is no doubt he will be greatly missed in the district.

The Derbyshire Courier May 11th 1915

The Hasland Silver Prize Band gave a sacred concert on Sunday evening in the Eastwood Park where a good selection of music was rendered under the conductor-ship of Mr H. T. Moseley. A collection in aid of the band funds realised £3-10-0d. Regarding the resignation of Mr Moseley as bandmaster, there appears to have been some misunderstanding. He has not, as yet, sent in his resignation and although working at Mansfield Colliery stated he hopes to maintain the position for some time.

The Derbyshire Courier Saturday 3rd June 1916

The village of Hasland was in a state of excitement on Friday night when a fire occurred on the premises occupied by Mr Hopkinson, Newsagent and Confectioner, Mansfield Road. It was the first big conflagration which had taken place since the burning down of the Co-operative Stores nearly sixteen years ago, although the Chesterfield Borough motor engine attended the same place a few years ago to quell a small fire in the roof. Mr and Mrs Hopkinson were in the house at about 11.20p.m. when one of the four children who was in bed became restless and called downstairs. On going upstairs Mr Hopkinson found considerable smoke in the bedroom, whilst about the same time Mr T. Cope, manager for Messrs. Woodhead whose premises are adjoining came to inform them that the place was on fire. Going through the shop it was found that the showroom above which was heavily stocked with toys, Stationary, etc. was ablaze so much so that they could not get into the roof for the smoke and heat. After vainly endeavouring to obtain the mastery by means of water conveyed in buckets the Borough Fire Brigade was summoned by telephone. Under the supervision of Inspector J. Fisher they were quickly on the scene with the motor engine, and two patent extinguishers not having the desired effect a standard was fixed near the Co-operative Stores and a good supply of water directed on the burning room which had got good hold. Eventually their efforts were rewarded and the outbreak extinguished, the Brigade being able to return to headquarters soon after 1 o'clock. Almost the whole of the stock in the room was destroyed in addition to which the doors of the two bedrooms were badly charred and the ceiling of the showroom damaged. It was fortunate that the discovery was made at the time stated for there is no doubt that had it gone a little longer loss of lives through suffocation would have taken place. How the fire originated is a mystery but it is surmised that it started between the ceiling of the shop and the floorboards of the destroyed room when the constant heat from the gas below and the warm weather caused the ignition. Matches were also stored in the roof but whether these had any connection with the outbreak it is impossible to say. The damage was estimated at about £150.

The Derbyshire Courier Saturday 24th June 1916

A cricket match was played on the New Inn ground, Winsick on Saturday, the object of which was to augment the funds of the Hasland and Winsick Soldiers Recognition Committees. Teams were chosen by the respective committees and an exciting game resulted in a tie of 52 runs each. For Hasland Mr A. Knight was top scorer with 19 whilst Mr Wilfred Copping had this honour for the home side with 23 not out. Messrs G. H. Matthews and D. Mycock were the umpires.

The Derbyshire Courier Saturday 15th July 1916

An unusual accident occurred in Hasland Road on Saturday afternoon. A horse and milk float belonging to Mr Frank Parker of Manor House Farm, Winsick, in charge of a youth named Charles Neale was on the way to Penmore Isolation Hospital to deliver milk. When about to turn into the hospital lane the driver pulled up to allow the 5.30 Hasland Motor Bus to pass, and whilst waiting the animal grew restless with the result that it got one of it s fore feet under the hind wheel of the car. The hoof was practically cut off causing considerable pain to the horse which was destroyed as soon as possible and conveyed to Chesterfield.

The Derbyshire Courier Saturday 15th July 1916

Mr Ernest Hoades son of Mr Isaac Hoades, Grocer, Mansfield Road, Winsick, was the victim of an accident in Chesterfield on Friday afternoon. He had pulled up his horse and dray near Mr Pilley's shop in Central Pavement and was about to examine a broken shoe on one of the animals feet, when through some cause it kicked out. In trying to avoid a kick Hoades caught his head with great violence underneath the shaft sustaining a serious cut on the head. He was removed to the borough police station where first aid was rendered. Afterwards he was conveyed to Chesterfield Hospital where several stitches were inserted.

The Derbyshire Courier Saturday 23rd September 1916

At Chesterfield on Saturday Clifford Charlesworth was ordered to pay 6/- for damaging growing turnips of the value of 6d the property of Fred Smith at Hasland on the 31st August.

The Derbyshire Courier 14th October 1916

Report of the death of Mrs Hallam, 47yrs, wife of Mr John Hallam, Hampton Street, Hasland.
She was the second daughter of Mr Obadiah Allen one of the pioneers of Primitive Methodism in the village. She left a daughter Mary Hallam and a son Jack Hallam.

The Derbyshire Courier Saturday 4th November 1916

On behalf of the Trust Fund of The Hasland Primitive Methodist Church a tea was provided in the schoolroom on Wednesday by the members of the Sunday School staff and about 60 persons sat down. A social evening followed when songs were given by Mrs W. Hudson, duets by Misses Marie and May Hall, with Mrs M. Hall as accompanist, whilst pianoforte duets were also given by Misses Eva and

Gwendoline Hudson.

The Derbyshire Courier 24th March 1917

Mr D. Knight presided over a well attended meeting of garden holders in the Hasland Workingmen s Institute on Wednesday. Mr T. J. Nelson (Ashgate) gave a lecture on allotments in which he dealt especially with the cultivation of new plots. The lecture was highly appreciated and should prove useful to the many aspirants to cultivation. The village is quite alive to the situation, building sites and various fields having been acquired recently and the interest manifested by the working men after their days toil is indeed encouraging.

The Derbyshire Courier Saturday 8th September 1917

A familiar figure in the Hasland and Grassmoor district in the person of Mr William Gilding of Churchside Farm, Hasland, passed away under sad circumstances on Tuesday. He was in his usual health when he turned out with his horse and cart in the morning to follow his duties as Scavenging Contractor to the Hasland Parish Council but whilst loading his vehicle in New Street, Grassmoor he was the victim of an apoplectic seizure. He was carried into the house of Mr S. Rushton. Medical aid was summoned and in the afternoon he was conveyed to his home where despite all attention, passed away at 9 to10pm without regaining consciousness. Mr Gilding who was 70 years of age and had lived in the district the whole of his life was born at Churchside Farm which has been occupied by members of the family for several generations. Upon his marriage he went to live at Grasshill and took possession of the farm upon the retirement of his uncle Mr W. Hall well over 29 years ago. The interment is to take place at Hasland Cemetery this (Saturday) afternoon.

The Derbyshire Courier 15th September 1917
DAMAGE IN PUBLIC PARKS
FLOGGING FOR A HASLAND BOY

Wicked damage to saplings in Eastwood Park, Hasland by the cutting away of the bark with knives was the subject of a complaint at Chesterfield Borough Police Court on Monday. Jasper Barlow, 8, of York Street, Hasland was summoned for causing damage exceeding £1. The Town Clerk Mr J. H. Rothwell prosecuting said he regretted having to bring a boy of such tender years before the court but the amount of damage that was going on in Eastwood Park and other parts of the borough was such that the authorities were compelled to bring the case before them as a warning to the offenders. There were 23 saplings in Eastwood Park the barks of which had been cut with a knife. Defendant admitted having cut 13 of them and the damage done was at least £1. It was a serious offence and one that might be committed for trial were the boy not of such tender years. There was one remedy which he urged should be adopted and that was whipping. It was within the power of the bench to order the boy 6 strokes with the birch rod and the view of the parks committee was that such punishment was the best means of stopping such abominable conduct. It was very difficult for anyone to catch the offenders for the damage was done when there was no-one about. Much of the damage that was suffered in the public parks was never found out. The saplings were presented by Alderman G. A. Eastwood and were planted only on the 5th April. P.C. Johnson said the cutting on some of the trees extended over 2 inches. There were notice boards in the park warning boys against such conduct. Charles Skidmore, Park Keeper, said the trees were valuable ones and the damage was considerably more than £1. Mr W. Jacques (chairman) ordering the mother of the boy to pay the costs of the prosecution and directing that the boy received six strokes with the birch rod said the bench hoped it would be a warning not only to the defendant but to other boys who did such stupid and silly damage in the parks. It is time it was stopped said Mr Jacques. We have threatened what we will do and we are going to carry it out by giving you a flogging.

The Derbyshire Times Saturday January 11th 1918
RELIC OF A BYGONE AGE
ONE OF CHESTERFIELD S TWO THATCHED HOUSES

The Whirlygig of time has brought with it many changes and of the ancient straw-thatched cottages which used to abound in the Chesterfield district only two have survived the demand for modern building sites, wider streets and improved sanitary conditions, one in Old Road and the other in Chapel Street, Hasland.

The Derbyshire Times Saturday 19th January 1918

Much sympathy will be felt for Mr and Mrs W. H. Slinn, the postmaster and post-mistress at Hasland, in the loss of their eldest daughter. The girl, Edna, was a clever girl, 15 years of age and had attended the Hasland Church Schools where she had won a minor scholarship tenable at the Girl s High School, Chesterfield. She was in the Chesterfield Hospital at the time of her death which occurred through peritonitis following an operation. At the funeral on Sunday the Reverend W. Vivian Davies officiated. Captain Peck attended on behalf of the local Girl Guides as did Miss Munro of the High School, Mr W, Wilbourne and Mrs Bunting, the teachers and scholars of the Senior Sunday School.

The Derbyshire Courier Saturday 2nd March 1918
MR ARTHUR SAXTON

The good work accomplished on behalf of the Hasland Primitive Methodist Church by the late Mr Arthur Saxton of Matlock and formerly of Hasland was eulogised on Sunday afternoon when a marble tablet to his memory was unveiled. The Rev. G. Ford presided and Mr C. Barlow gave a resume of Mr Saxton's active interest in the church and circuit. The unveiling ceremony was performed by Mr John Ball who had known Mr Saxton from childhood when they both lived at Ling's Row. Mr Ball said credit was due to Mr Saxton for the position he attained in public life for as boys they had no schooling except that of the Sunday School which was then held in a small cottage and from which in addition to the man whose memory they had met to honour emanated such men as the Reverend S. S. Henshaw (a past president of the P.M. Conference) the Reverend G. O. Lee (who is still in the ministry in America) and the Reverend Mr Nuttall formerly of Tibshelf. The speaker appealed to the Sunday School teachers to continue in their good work and not be disappointed if they did not see the result of their labours for these would undoubtedly follow.

The Derbyshire Courier January 1st 1921

Permission has been refused for Mr D. Redgrave to convert an army hut into a blacksmith's shop adjoining Eastwood Park.

The Derbyshire Courier January 1st 1921

A ball was held in the Village Hall, Hasland on Monday. The M.C.'s were Messrs H. Ripon, J. Riley, Blackburn and Cheetham. The music was provided by Ripper's Band.

The Derbyshire Courier January 1st 1921

A Christmas Party took place in the Primitive Methodist Schoolroom, Hasland on Wednesday. A Christmas tree was stripped and the gifts distributed. Entertainment was provided by Miss A. Alton (contralto), Mr T. Sharpe (humorist), and Mr J. Hill (ventriloquist). The proceeds are in aid of the forthcoming Bazaar.

The Derbyshire Courier January 15th 1921

A movement is on foot in Hasland to make a presentation to Miss H. E. Hollingworth late Headmistress of the Infant's Church School who recently retired after being a teacher over 50 years. The idea originated among many of her former scholars and striking evidence of her popularity is furnished by the fact that approximately £120 has been raised by a canvass of the village. The intention of the promoters is to make a personal presentation to Miss Hollingworth of an address on vellum.

The Derbyshire Courier January 22nd 1921
RUN OVER BY TRAIN
HASLAND RAILWAY GUARD S FATAL SLIP

Richmond Short (64) Railway Guard, of Loco Terrace, Park Hill, Hasland was instantly killed whilst working on the Midland Railway on Monday afternoon by being run over by a coal train in the Black Shale Sidings of the Grassmoor Colliery Sidings.

The Derbyshire Courier January 22nd 1921

Mr W. Hollingworth the clerk to Hasland parish Council, at the monthly meeting on Tuesday, said it may be taken for granted that the Chesterfield Rural District Council had granted the application made by James Gilding, the carting contractor to Hasland Parish Council, for an advance of 5/- a day. The increase, it was pointed out, would amount to £78 a year which was equal to a rate of a penny in the pound. They would however, have the satisfaction of knowing they were not paying it for nothing said a member (Mr T. Whitmore).

The Derbyshire Courier Saturday January 29th 1921
BESIEGED LORRY
HASLAND SEQUEL TO MINER'S PRACTICE
A FATAL FALL

In alighting from a motor lorry as it was travelling at about 12 miles an hour, Isaiah Marriott (37) a married man of Hoole Street, Hasland, fell on his face and fractured his skull. He died from his injuries at Chesterfield Royal Hospital. The lorry which belonged to the British Petroleum Company was carrying a tank containing 660 gallons of petrol. It was driven by Ernest William Hall, 32 Beetwell Street, Chesterfield.

At the inquest on Monday Cecil Rowland, Hoole Street, Hasland said Marriott, who was a rope splicer employed at Williamthorpe Colliery, scrambled onto the back of the lorry together with himself and 11 other men returning home from work when the driver pulled up at Bond s Main on Wednesday afternoon last week to pick up a man he knew. There were about 15 men on the lorry altogether. Marriott wanted to get off at the junction of Calow Lane and Mansfield Road, but the lorry was travelling at from 15 to 20 miles an hour. One of the men shouted to those on the front to tell the driver to slow down, and a man called Fullwood who was riding in the cab said the driver would not stop. Marriott then tried to get off. He got onto his feet safely and then ran for about three yards holding onto the back of the lorry. On releasing his hold, he fell face downwards onto the road. The lorry continued it's journey and did not pull up until near Penmore House when the driver was compelled to slow down because of the other traffic.

SAID NOTHING TO DRIVER

Witness then got off but did not say anything to the driver about Marriott's fall because he thought the man had possibly only stunned himself. On going back he found Marriott lying unconscious by the side of the road where he had been carried by two men. He was taken into the surgery of Dr. Ford and then in a taxi-cab to Chesterfield Royal Hospital. He died early on Friday morning. Cross-examined by Mr B. Mather, who represented the driver, witness admitted that they were not invited to ride on the lorry and that they were taking a risk in doing so. The tank made it impossible for the driver to see who were at the back but he must have known they were there because he shouted to them 'Don't smoke because of the petrol'. He did not think the driver knew anything of the accident until he got to Chesterfield. It was a common practice for miners coming from Bond's Main to jump on passing motor lorries in order to get home earlier. The Coroner (Dr. A. Green) said 'Don't you think it was a rash thing to do, to get off a lorry going at 15 miles an hour?' 'Yes sir'. Ephraim Fullwood, James Street, Stonegravels, Chesterfield, who got on the front of the lorry when his mate was invited by the driver to do so, said that when the other men scrambled on the back, the driver told them it would be best for them not to get on. The driver was afraid of the petrol, and when the men did not get off he told them not to smoke or strike matches. When some more miners tried to scramble onto the back and sides and back of the lorry near Grassmoor Station, the driver told them to keep off and said he would not stop at Hasland. Witness communicated this warning to the men who were on. He did not hear anybody call out at Hasland for the driver to pull up but he (witness) told him to do so. Answering the Coroner, witness said the driver might have thought the men were going to Chesterfield. Ernest William Hall, the driver of the lorry, said he did not think there was anybody on the back of the lorry after he warned the men to get off at Grassmoor Station. They're a nuisance he added.

George Marriott, the father of deceased suggested that the accident was the result of foolhardiness on the part of the driver in trying to take the men through to Chesterfield so that they would have to walk back again. In reply to Mr Mather, Hall said the men at the back of the lorry had not his authority to ride. There were 660 gallons of petrol in the tank and he warned the men of the consequence if anything happened. The lorry was not travelling at more than 12 miles an hour. The Coroner said it was apparently an impossibility for the driver to get rid of the men. The driver appeared to have done all he could to prevent them from getting on the lorry but they did not heed the warning and rode at their own risk. A verdict of accidental death was returned.

The Derbyshire Courier February 5th 1921

Under the auspices of the Hasland Green Tennis Club, a Grand Ball took place in the Village Hall on Wednesday. The M.C.'s were Messrs. E. Gouridge and W. Parker. Prothero's Band supplied the music.

The Derbyshire Times June 25th 1921
LIVELINESS AT HASLAND

Up to this week the miners in Hasland had been very quiet, but on Tuesday there was considerable liveliness. During the morning several carts were stopped and their loads of outcrop coal upset, and it was not long before this coal had been cleared away by those short of fuel. One well known carting contractor Mr W. Oakley, had his cart tipped up in the centre of the village. It is alleged that someone in the crowd struck him. Another man with a dray loaded with bags of coal burst into tears but his coal and bags were not long in disappearing. Empty vehicles going down Calow Lane were stopped and their drivers turned back. Headings of the workings in a field down Calow Lane, locally known as the 'Gorse Field' were knocked down and dirt thrown into the shaft. At night a procession was formed and a good number went to Grassmoor and considerable excitement prevailed there. The outcrop workers were ready with pick and shovel but no personal damage was done, although the workings came in for some rough handling.

The Derbyshire Times August 6th 1921
YEOMAN KILLED AT SHOWGROUND

During a military tournament at Chesterfield and East Derbyshire Agricultural Show at Eastwood Park, Hasland on Wednesday, one of the riders was thrown from his horse and killed instantaneously. The fatality was witnessed by a crowd of 4,000 spectators. The tournament was abandoned. The rider was Trooper Joseph Gyte (42) married of Wheatbridge Road, Brampton, a member of the Sherwood Rangers Yeomanry by whom the tournament was being given. He was one of six competitors in an individual tent pegging competition. After missing the peg on the first time round he was making his second attempt with the horse galloping, when his lance became entangled between the animal's front legs. To the horror of the spectators, both the horse and rider were thrown. The hind quarters of the horse fell across the rider and he was killed instantly. Trooper Gyte was an old soldier and he served in the Yeomanry 22 years. He was a first class rider and served for the full period of the War, with his Regiment at one time being attached to the Machine Gun Corps.

Tent pegging was no new experience to him he had frequently taken part in competitions at the regimental camps as recently as Monday, when he was successful at a contest at Newark. Coming to Chesterfield as a boy he drove the Post Office Horse Mail at an early age for Mr Richard Kirk. By trade he was an iron turner employed at the engineering works of Bryan Donkin Company, Chesterfield. He leaves a widow and five children

The Derbyshire Times March 4th 1922
HASLAND CINEMA LTD.

Hasland Cinema Ltd. has been registered with a capital of £6,000 in £1.00 shares to carry on business as a cinema proprietor. Minimum cash subscriptions in case of first offer of shares to the public £1,500. The first directors are J. B. Cutts, 'Holmewood', Avenue Road, Whittington Moor, H. Cropper, 'Gladstone Villa', Hasland, T. S. Wilcockson, 'Glencoe House', Hasland (architect), E. E. Glassbrook, Doe Lea (provision merchant), G. L. Swift, 'Fairhaven', Chesterfield, F. Haslam, Doncaster (builder). Qualification £250. Renumeration £25 each per annum. Secretary, C. H. Yates, registered office, Knifesmith Gate, Chesterfield.

The Derbyshire Times Saturday August 5th 1922
HASLAND, GRASSMOOR, BOND'S MAIN & DISTRICT

It is hoped that the Miner's Welfare Scheme for Hasland will take the form of Public Baths if a suitable site centrally can be obtained and if the Corporation can be induced to take over the maintenance of the Baths after erection. With a view to putting the scheme before the Corporation a deputation from the Hasland Committee were appointed to interview the Chairman of the Health Committee (Ald. Edmunds) on Friday evening.

The Derbyshire Times Saturday August 19th 1922

News is to hand that Bernard Holleworth the 11 year old son of Mr W. H.

100

Holleworth of Hampton Street, Hasland has won a Heathcote Scholarship tenable at the Chesterfield Grammar School for 4 years. Holleworth is now a pupil at the Church Schools under Mr B. C. Boden.

The Derbyshire Times Saturday September 23rd 1922

On Monday a motor car belonging to Mr Burton, Hasland Road mounted the pavement at the corner of Devonshire Avenue and collided with a lamp-post. The post was snapped clean in two, and the car was also damaged. Before night a new lamp-post had been erected.

The Derbyshire Times Saturday September 23rd 1922

Much interest has been taken this weekend in the erection of the beautiful War Memorial to the men of Hasland which will be unveiled in Eastwood Park on Sunday afternoon by the Mayor of Chesterfield (Alderman Rhodes). The Corporation will attend with Regalia. The Memorial will be dedicated by the Reverend Vivian Davies, Rector of Hasland, who must be getting quite an expert in these dedicatory services. We believe this will be the sixth memorial that the Rector has dedicated.

The Derbyshire Times Saturday October 7th 1922

After being closed for several weeks for renovation the P.M.Church, Hasland was reopened on Sunday. Special services were held with Mr N.Grainger preaching in the morning. In the afternoon there was a special musical service. The soloists were Miss Chapman and Mr Sharratt and the Chairman Ald.G.A.Eastwood. In the evening Mr J.W.Lee was the preacher. All the collections were for the Renovation Fund.

The Derbyshire Times Friday 19th May 1944
OBITUARY – MR J. HALLAM

Known locally as 'Honest John' Mr John Hallam, 81, died suddenly at his home Hampton Street, Hasland, Chesterfield on Sunday. For over 40 years Mr Hallam had conducted a hardware business at his home. He formerly worked at the Hasland Loco Sheds. He had almost 60 years association with Hasland Primitive Methodist Church being a trustee and treasurer for 40 years. He leaves a son and a daughter the latter being the wife Mr M. Cox, hairdresser, Chesterfield.

Hasland Methodist Church was full at the service preceding the interment at Hasland Cemetery on Wednesday.

The Derbyshire Times Friday 1st April 1949
GOLDEN WEDDING MR AND MRS J. C. JACKSON, HASLAND

Two well-known workers for the Methodist cause in Hasland will on Sunday celebrate their Golden wedding Anniversary. They are Mr and Mrs J. C. Jackson, Hampton Street, Hasland both natives of Leicestershire who came to this district in 1897. They were married at the old Methodist Church, Chapel Street, Hasland on April 3rd 1899 and have three sons. Mr John Charles JACKSON who is 72 worked for 25 years at the Grassmoor Colliery, nine of them as a deputy and later worked as an agent for the Pearl Assurance Company. Before his retirement in 1943 he was employed for 14 years by the Bryan Donkin Company. He was for many years a Sunday School teacher and superintendent of the Hasland Methodist Church of which he is still a trustee. His wife Dorothy who is 73 was for 23 years also a Sunday School teacher at the Church. She has been a member of the Borough Welfare Committee and the Nursing Association for over 30 years.
A special party to which 40 guests have been invited will be held in honour of the occasion at the Methodist Schoolroom on April 9th.

The Derbyshire Times Friday March 18th 1955
HASLAND, GRASSMOOR, BOND'S MAIN & DISTRICT
56 YEARS IN COLLIERIES, MR A. E. LITTLEWOOD M.B.E.,
HASLAND DIES AT 74

Mr Albert Edward Littlewood 74, 'Thornbank', Broomfield Avenue, Hasland who was awarded the M.B.E. in 1948 for outstanding service to the mining industry and who retired in 1950 after 56 years in the industry, died at Scarsdale Hospital on Saturday. Mr Littlewood was a native of West Bromwich. At the age of 14 he entered the mining industry as a haulage boy at Treeton Colliery and subsequently became a deputy there. He moved to Holmewood in 1914 joining the Hardwick Colliery Company as a deputy. He was appointed under-manager on the deep hard seam of Williamthorpe in 1931 and was in charge when the pit was mechanised in 1936. From 1927 to 1940 he taught mining science at Holmewood Evening School. He resigned as under-manager in 1940 and was presented with an Illuminated Address by the staff and workmen of the Hardwick Colliery Company. The Address believed to be the only one of it's kind presented in the country was a mark of appreciation for his service to the Company. Several men including Mr J. S. Raynor (area production manager N. E. Division N.C.B.) and Mr W. A. Wood (divisional safety engineer) who have since become prominent officials of the N.C.B. served their studentship under Mr Littlewood.

Mr Littlewood returned from retirement in 1940 to take the position of training officer under the N.C.B. at Williamthorpe, a position held until his final retirement in 1950.

Mr Littlewood had played a prominent part in social activities in the Holmewood district. He had been chairman of Holmewood Operatic Society, a member of Heath and Williamthorpe Corporative Society Committee and of Hardwick Band Committee. He was also a member of the Royal Alfred Lodge of Freemasons, Alfreton. Bereaved are a widow, two sons and one daughter. The funeral took place at Hasland on Wednesday, a service at St.Paul's Church being conducted by the Rev. C. N. Lavender.

The Derbyshire Times Friday 23rd April 1965
DEATH AT 90 OF MR F. J. BALL, HASLAND

Mr Francis John Ball (90) Hampton Street, Hasland died at his home on Thursday week. Most of his working life was spent as a fireman at Grassmoor Colliery retiring 20 years ago. He was a member for over half a century of Hasland Working Men's Club being made an honorary member and he was an old member of the Nottingham Unity of Oddfellows. He had a life-long association with Hasland Methodist Church and was for many years a choir member in addition to being a Sunday School teacher and secretary for a few years. His wife died three years ago and he leaves a son and a daughter. The service at Hasland Methodist Church on Tuesday conducted by Sister Elizabeth Gillings was followed by interment in Hasland Cemetery. Miss E. Johnson was organist.

HASLAND'S 83 HEROES

A MEMORIAL ERECTED IN EASTWOOD PARK

The figure of a soldier in active service, dressed and worked in white marble standing on a plinth, resting on tiers of stone, now marks Hasland's tribute to the memory of 83 of it's sons who fell in the Great War. Erected on a prominent site at the entrance to Eastwood Park, it has the following inscription '1914 - 1918 To the glorious memory of the men of this part of the Township of Hasland who gave their lives in the cause of God, King and Country. Their deeds live after them. Faithful unto death'. Around the sides the names of the men who paid the supreme sacrifice are engraved.

The unveiling ceremony took place on Sunday when in the presence of several thousand people, the Mayor, Alderman W. Rhodes, pulled a cord which drew aside the folds of the Union Jack that surrounded the memorial. Wearing his mayoral robes and chain of office he was accompanied by the Deputy Mayor, Alderman W. Hawksley Edmunds, Alderman G. A. Eastwood who also presided over the gathering, and the Town Clerk, Mr J. H. Rothwell.

At each corner of the memorial a Sergeant of the 6th Sherwood Foresters was posted with the muzzle of his rifle resting on his boot, while on either side were grouped a firing party and buglers from the same unit. Special places were roped off to accommodate the many relatives and friends of the fallen, and then behind all these stood the large gathering in which every local organisation and institution was represented.

The Mayor having unveiled the memorial, the momentary silence was broken by the melancholy strains of the 'Last Post' followed by the sharp echoes of three volleys by the firing party.

A word of praise must be given to the organisers of Sunday's ceremonial, it was excellently done. There was no hitch in the long procession made up of many units, which was formed and marshalled in the park in a manner which would have done credit to a trained military assembly. The bands taking part in the procession from the Eyre Street Schools were: Hasland Silver Prize Band, Chesterfield Town and Comrades Band, The United Services Band and the Boy Scouts Band. Ex-service-men from Chesterfield, Hasland, Winsick and Grassmoor were present in large numbers, together with the Hasland Ambulance Corps and the Committees of the Workingmen's Clubs of Hasland, Grassmoor and Bond s Main. Amongst other parties present were the Hasland Parish Council, the Local Lodges of the Druids, Oddfellows, Pure Order of Britons, Boy Scouts and Girl Guides.

The Mayor complimented the people of Hasland upon having erected such a beautiful memorial to the memory of those who died in helping to preserve intact the safety and liberty of the Country. It would stand as an inspiration to them to realise that duty was the first obligation they owed, not only to themselves, but to their Country. But the fixing of a memorial to keep fresh in their minds the names of the fallen, ought not to end the obligations of the people, for they had to continue that sympathy and help to the wives and dependants who were left behind.

Dedicatory prayers were said by the Reverend W. V. Davies, Rector of Hasland, whilst the lesson was read by the Reverend C. A. Page. Hymns were sung at intervals and the Hasland Primitive Methodist Choir gave the chorus Homeland .

Bereaved relatives and friends placed wreaths at the base of the memorial which was soon covered with beautiful floral tributes, not the least effective being the bunches of flowers brought by the little children whose fathers and brothers fell in the Great War. An impressive service concluded with the sounding of 'The Reveille' by the buglers.

The memorial was executed by A. Allsop, sculptor, Eyre Street, Chesterfield.

The Derbyshire Times 30th September 1922.

The Cenotaph, Eastwood Park, Hasland.

WE WILL REMEMBER THEM

SOLDIERS FROM HASLAND WHO WERE KILLED IN THE GREAT WAR WHOSE NAMES ARE ON THE HASLAND CENOTAPH

ALLEN - ALBERT
APPLEYARD - HARRY
ARNOLD - ARTHUR FREDERICK
ASKEY - ALFRED HENRY
ATTENBOROUGH - JOHN
ATTENBOROUGH - JABEZ
BAMFORD - THOMAS BENJAMIN
BAILEY - GEORGE
BENNETT - ROBERT FREDERICK
BLAND - BERNARD JAMES
BOOTH - PERCY ARTHUR
BRADLEY - JAMES
BRADLEY - WILLIAM
BROWN - JOHN
BUCKLES - JOHN
BURNHAM - JOSEPH
BUTT - KENNETH
CHAMBERLAIN - WILLIAM
COCKETT - WILLIAM ARTHUR
COWLEY - HERBERT HAROLD
DAY - ALBERT VICTOR
DAVIDSON - JOHN W.
DEACON - CECIL F.
DEAKIN - THOMAS HARRY
DUMELOW - WILLIAM HENRY
DUMELOW - CHARLES
EDWARDS - WILLIAM THOMAS
FISHER - GEORGE HENRY
GEORGE -WILLIAM HENRY
GILDING - JAMES
GOODWIN - ARTHUR
GOODWIN - HARRY
GRAHAM - WILLIAM HARRY
GUEST - JOHN THOMAS
HANCOCK - ALBERT WILLIAM
HEATH - J. ROLAND
HOOLE - BERNARD C.
HOPKINSON - WILLIAM H.

MELLOR - WILLOUGHBY
MELLOR - JOHN
MELLOR - ERNEST
MELLOR - WILFRED
METCALF - FRED
MITSON - WILLIAM
MOAKES - OLIVER
MYCOCK - ARNOLD
ORGAN - FREDERICK JOHN
PADBURY - GEORGE
PELL - JOHN
PENN - ALBERT
PICKERING - THOMAS E.
RAWSON - SAMUEL HILL
RAYBOULD - WILLIAM
RIGGOTT - JAMES
RUFF - WILLIAM T.
ROWLAND - ALBERT
RUMSEY - JAMES
RUSH - GEORGE FREDERICK
SCOTT - HARRY
SIMMONS - HENRY
SULMAN - THOMAS WILLIAM
TRUEMAN - STANLEY
TURLEY - BERT
UNWIN - WILLIAM MANFRED
VERO - TOM
WALKER - JAMES COXON
WALKER - FREDERICK
WIDDOWSON - JOHN
WILLIAMS - WALTER T.
WILSON - GEORGE HARRY
WOOLLEY - WILFRED
WHITE - JOHN

HOLLINGWORTH - CHARLES CUTHBERT
HOLLINGWORTH - GEORGE
HOLLAND - JAMES
HOLLAND - DANIEL
HUTCHBY - ARTHUR
ILIFFE - STANLEY
JONES - ROBERT IBALL
JENKINSON - HAROLD JAMES
KENT - ALBERT HENRY
KEIGHTLEY - THOMAS
LYNN - WALTER CYRIL
MARSH - ERNEST ALBERT

INFORMATION ON THE DEATHS
OF SOME OF THESE SOLDIERS

The Derbyshire Courier Tuesday May 11th 1915
THE COUNTY S LOSSES IN KILLED AND WOUNDED
PRIVATE BRADLEY – HASLAND

Much sympathy is felt with Mr and Mrs W. Bradley of York Street, Hasland in the loss they have sustained by the death of their eldest son James. Deceased, who attained his majority only a month ago enlisted in the Royal Marines last November and was drafted out on 1st March to the Dardanelles. He was attached to HMS Franconia and on Wednesday evening his parents were notified by the Admiralty that he had succumbed to wounds in hospital in Alexandria on Monday.

Prior to his enlistment he followed the occupation of butcher. He began his apprenticeship with Mr J. Gothard, York Street and later was in service to Mr Frank Lowe, Mansfield Road. He was a much respected member of St. Paul's Church.

The Derbyshire Courier 10th July 1915
ANOTHER HASLAND MAN'S FATE

It has been rumoured for some time that Pte. Kenneth Butt, of the Midland Cottages, Hasland, has been missing, and now official news has arrived with his father Mr Harry Butt, the local secretary of the N.U.R., that his son has been missing since May 9th 'Place not stated'. The young man was only 18 years old, and joined the Notts. and Derbys. soon after the War commenced and was trained at Whitley Bay. Before going to the Front he had only one short leave last Christmas when he came home. A railway man's son, he was one of the number who joined the regiment about the same time, and they all seem to have been pretty well in the thick of it. These were Privates W. Edwards, C. Presgrave and Mellor (all killed). George J. Hone, A. Kent (wounded) and Penn and Allen who seem so far to have escaped harm. Before joining the Forces, Kenneth Butt worked at Clay Cross No 9 pit and had worked previous to that at the Storforth Lane Brick Works, Grassmoor Collieries and Holmewood Collieries. He was a member of Hasland Church. His brother William, who joined the 3rd/6th Sherwoods about four months ago is still training in Chesterfield.

The Derbyshire Times 13th November 1915
HASLAND MAN KILLED

Private Percy Arthur Booth who lived with his parents at Calow Lane, Hasland has met his death in The Dardanelles. He was in a regiment that has seen a lot of fighting in that hot corner of the earth, the 1st Lancashire Fusiliers. He joined the Leicestershires in the first place a fortnight after the War began then he was transferred to the Notts. And Derbys. and sent to Newcastle and after a short furlough at home was sent to the Dardanelles in August this year with the Lancashire Fusiliers. On Saturday morning his parents received a letter from the authorities stating that their son died on October 30th whilst undergoing the operation of having his right leg removed. In one of his recent letters home Pte.Booth wrote he was in hopes of having his feet under the table for Christmas. He was 32 years of age and was employed for a time at the Grassmoor Collieries. Previous to that he had been a hairdresser in Hasland and Whittington Moor. He had two brothers with the forces, Harold in the Sheffield City Battalion of the Yorks. and Lancs., and John Thomas in the South Staffords.

The Derbyshire Times 11th December 1915
KILLED ON HIS BIRTHDAY

By a peculiar coincidence a letter was delivered on Saturday morning to Mr and Mrs Turley, Churchside, Hasland from their son in France Pte.Bert Turley, Sherwood Foresters and the same post brought two letters from his friends stating he had been killed on the day he wrote the letter. Pte.Turley was 22 years of age on the day he was killed. His father is a well-known driver on the Midland Railway. Turley was a member of Hasland Church and also attended the Brotherhood in the village. Previous to enlisting in August last year he was at Holmewood Colliery. He was I stationed at Backworth and then at Whitley Bay and went to the Front on August 16th 1915.

The Derbyshire Courier Saturday 4th March 1916
A HASLAND LOSS
VICTIM OF EARLY MORNING BOMBARDMENT

After a lengthy immunity from casualties Hasland this week mourns the loss of another of it's gallant sons in the person of Pte. Sam Hill Rawson of the 8th Lincolnshire Regiment who was killed in action in France on 23rd February. The news was conveyed to Mr and Mrs Charles Hill of Kent Street, Hasland (who took to the unfortunate soldier on the death of his grandmother Mrs Rawson of Winsick with whom he formerly resided ten years ago) in a letter from Lance Corporal J. W.

Potter of the same regiment, also a Hasland lad, dated 23rd February in which he states that Pte. Rawson was killed during a bombardment of their trench at 5 o'clock that morning. He saw that the poor fellow was wrapped in a blanket and all done for him that was possible in the circumstances. In conclusion Lance Corporal Potter says 'All the boys wish to express their regret and offer their sincere sympathy in the loss sustained.' The news was confirmed in a communication received on Monday and dated 24th February from Rev. E. O. Clifford, Chaplain who informed Mr and Mrs Hill that he conducted the funeral service. He also arranged to have a cross erected over the grave of one who has given his life for his country.

The deceased soldier who was 22 years of age was of a most cheerful disposition well liked by all the young fellows of the village and the news of his death in action was received with much regret. He enlisted in the Lincolns on 29th August. He was joined soon afterwards by several more Hasland lads several of whom came to grief in the great battle of Loos on 25th September 1915. After training at various camps he was drafted to France early in September 1915 and for a considerable time has been attached to the Machine Gun Section. Previous to enlistment he worked at the Grassmoor Collieries.

The Derbyshire Courier 9th May 1916
SUNKEN SUBMARINE
HASLAND MEN ABOARD THE E22

Considerable anxiety is caused to two Hasland families as a result of the Admiralty announcement issued last weekend that the submarine E22 had been sunk in the North Sea and that only two of the crew had been saved.

P.O. Frederick John Organ only son of Mr and Mrs F. J. Organ of Hampton Street, and Stoker William Dumelow son of Mr and Mrs J. Dumelow of Park Hill, were aboard the submarine and whilst hopes are entertained by the parents of both men, it is probable that they have been lost in the service of their King and country. The parents are anxiously awaiting news as to whether the worst has befallen them. Frederick John Organ who is 29 years of age, and married at Dovercourt about a year ago a nurse at the Old Brompton Military Hospital, Chatham, was a scholar at the Hasland National School under the late Mr John Howell. He completed has education at the Chesterfield Grammar School after which he was apprenticed to the engineering trade at Messrs. Brian Donkin Ltd, Chesterfield. Upon completion of his 7 years term he continued for a little while in the employ of the firm and then joined the navy in 1910 as an engine room artificer. In this department he was very successful gradually rising to the position of second engineer, which post he was filling on the E22. Since the outbreak of war he has seen service on many battleships and cruisers and was on H.M.S.Garry when they sunk a German submarine off the north coast of Scotland. He volunteered for submarine service and was transferred from H.M.S. Garry to the E4 and about Christmas from that vessel to the E22.

Before joining the Navy P.O.Organ was an ardent footballer and for several seasons assisted the Hasland Football Club as right half back a position in which he had few superiors in the district. He was a member of the Hasland Church Institute and also of the St. Paul's Church. Of a cheery disposition he won the respect of all with whom he came in contact and his many friends in the locality only hope he could have the good fortune to be one of the two members of the crew saved.

The Derbyshire Courier Saturday 3rd June 1916
HASLAND

The many friends of Petty Officer F. J. Organ only son of Mr and Mrs Organ of Hampton Street, Hasland who was on the ill-fated submarine E22 will regret to learn that his parents have received a communication from the Admiralty intimating that their son was not one of the two men saved from the vessel. The hope was expressed that he might have the good fortune to be one of the rescued but as events turn out such is not the case. The sympathy of all Hasland residents is extended to Mr and Mrs Organ.

The Derbyshire Times Saturday 1st July 1916
HASLAND SAILOR DROWNED

Not until Tuesday did Mr and Mrs J. Dumelow of Loco Terrace, Hasland, Chesterfield receive definite news from the Admiralty that their second son First Class Stoker, William Henry Dumelow had gone down with the British submarine E22. He was 27 years of age and before entering the service of the Royal Navy 6 years ago he was a farmer being well-known in a wide area around Chesterfield his native town. Of fine physique he made good progress in the navy and when War was declared he was on a British cruiser which has the distinction of having fired the first shot in the campaign. He also engaged in the memorable battle of the Faukland Islands. Volunteering for under-craft work he was drafted to the E22 which at that time was one of the latest submarines.

Two of his brothers are with the forces, Private H. Dumelow who is with the Sherwoods in France and Corporal J. Dumelow of the Lincolnshire Artillery, he being in the East.

The Derbyshire Courier Saturday 22nd July 1916
HASLAND SOLDIER'S DEATH FROM WOUNDS

Another Hasland soldier has made the supreme sacrifice in the great drive, in the person of Private George Henry Fisher (20) of the Sherwood Foresters eldest son of Mr and Mrs Richard Fisher of Saunders Row, Hasland. News was received on Wednesday from the Army Records Department, Lichfield stating that Private Fisher died from wounds on the 2nd July. The deceased soldier was greatly respected by his comrades and a few months ago when sick in hospital his N.C.O Sergeant A. B. Farnsworth wrote to his parents stating how they missed his cheeriness and said he was the most courageous lad in the Company, always willing to do his part no matter how dangerous the work. Whilst in training he was the crack shot of his platoon and won a silver matchbox in a competition. Private Fisher enlisted on 29th August 1914, was drafted to France in August 1915, and formerly worked as a moulder at Sheepbridge Works. He was a valued member of the Hasland Troupe of Boy Scouts and was also a regular attender at St. Paul's Church Hasland. A singular coincidence is mentioned by Mrs Fisher who states that on 2nd July the very day her boy died she dreamt that he was dead.

The Derbyshire Courier Saturday 29th July 1916
HASLAND'S DOUBLE LOSS
BOY OF 17 DIES OF WOUNDS

This week Hasland mourns the loss of two more of it s gallant soldier sons who have made the supreme sacrifice.

Private Albert Allen (24), Sherwood Foresters, third son of Mr and Mrs Thomas Allen, Midland Terrace, Hasland was killed by being buried in a dug-out on the 5th July. The news was conveyed in a letter received by his brother Harry from one of his comrades Private E. Penn who also lives at The Midland Cottages, Hasland in which he says:

'I am very sorry to have to write this sad news to you but I think it my place to let you know that your brother Bert was killed in action on Wednesday 5th July. I did not see him killed myself but I was told after I came out of the charge that he was buried with five others in a dug-out. I am sorry to lose such a good pal, he was more like a brother to me. I had seen him while we were in the attack and he was still smiling. I hope your mother and father will not trouble too much over it as I know that he would not wish them to, for he has, like many others given his life for his King and Country. His pals in the Company wish me to express their deepest sympathy with you all in your sad loss. I have not been able to write before for I had to go into another attack and I am pleased to say I have come out alright again. We have been having some very heavy fighting but we have got him on the trot. Give my deepest sympathy to all at home.'

Private Allen enlisted on 3rd September 1914 and went to France on 16th March 1915. Formerly he was employed in The Dunston (No.2) Pit of The Grassmoor Colliery Company.

Private Tom Vero, Sherwood Foresters (Territorials) youngest son of Mrs T. Vero, Saunder's Terrace, Hasland joined the Army at the tender age of 17 years but as he was a big strong lad it would be quite easy for him to pass the authorities as much older. On Wednesday the sad news was received by his mother that he had died of wounds in France on 23rd July. Letters had been received stating that he had been wounded, one from M. A. C. Blair sister-in-charge of No.20 Clearing Station B.E.F. France dated 23rd July in which she said   I am sorry to inform you that your son Private Tom Vero was admitted into our station some days ago suffering from shell wounds to the left arm which has had to be amputated and lesser wounds. He left by train for the base, hoping you will soon have him home safely.

The other was from A. E. Haywood sister-in-charge of No.2 Ward No.2 Stationary Hospital, B.E.F. which stated that the unfortunate lad had been brought into her ward suffering very badly from wounds in the left arm both hips and thighs. She said 'The wounds were very severe and gangrenous and the doctors give very little hope for the poor laddie's life. He knows I am writing and sends his love. Poor little chap it seems so terrible for one so young. You must be quite sure everything possible will be done for him and I will let you know how he goes on.' These communications were followed by the following telegram from the Territorial Forces Records Depot, Lichfield on Wednesday 'Regret to inform you that 4105 Private Vero, Sherwood Foresters, died in No.2 Stationary Hospital, Abberville from gunshot wounds in thighs and arms on 23rd July.'

The sympathy of all Hasland residents is extended to Mrs Vero in her loss which seems more hard to bear from the fact that he was never allowed leave after he went to Grantham. He was even refused leave when sent for to attend the funeral of his eldest brother who died last October as a result of sustaining a broken leg in a local colliery. The deceased soldier who attained his 17th birthday only last February enlisted in the Territorials on 15th February 1915 and went to France on 24th October of the same year. Previous to joining the forces he was a Pony Driver in the Dunston (No.2) Pit of the Grassmoor Company.

The Derbyshire Times 26th August 1916
HASLAND HEROES

As we reported a fortnight ago Corporal Jack Attenborough has been wounded and missing since July 25th 1916. It is now feared that he has been killed as the following letter has been received from his Captain in The King's Rifles 'With regard to your enquiry after your brother. I am very sorry indeed to have to tell you that on the night of 25th July when proceeding in the trenches to go into action he was killed by shell fire. The enemy put up a heavy barrage and we were some time before we could go on. His death must have been instantaneous from what the men tell me who were close to him. Several were hit by the same shell. I was particularly sorry as he was an excellent fellow and a fine NCO and of great value to my Company.'

Corporal Attenborough joined the Army in the summer of 1915. He was formerly employed by the Grassmoor Colliery Co. and he was a valued member of Hasland Silver Prize Band. He was a member of the Regimental Band. He has a brother Charlie in the R.F.A. Jack, as he was called, was at one time blower at the Church in Hasland.

The Derbyshire Courier Saturday 26th August 1916
HASLAND'S FURTHER LOSSES

Sympathy is also extended to Mr and Mrs Thomas Bamford of Eyre Street, Hasland whose second son Private T. B. Bamford Scottish Battalion Kings Liverpool Regiment was killed in action in France on 9th August. Last week news was received from Private A. B. Wellings of 'L' gun section of the same regiment that Private Bamford was missing whilst intimation was received that he met his death in action, official news of which came from the War Office on Thursday morning. The Company Quarter-Master Sergeant J. Irving the deceased Soldier's non-commissioned officer has also written to the bereaved parents, in his letter he says 'You will have doubtlessly heard that your son Private T. Bamford has been killed in action. He was killed whilst taking part in an attack on the German trenches and I am taking this opportunity of expressing on behalf of your son's comrades, his Company Officer (Captain Jaeger) and myself our deepest sympathy with you. Pte. Bamford was always a good and conscientious soldier and his loss will be felt by all who knew him.'

Commencing his education at the Hasland National School Pte. Bamford at the age of 10 went to the Chesterfield Grammar School where he remained for 10 years He then went to a French school for languages for a year after which he obtained a position as junior master at Felixstowe College which post he held at the time of enlistment on 31st August 1915 being drafted to France on 24th December 1915.He was 25 years of age and a young man most respected by all with whom he came in contact and he will be sadly missed by his many friends in the district.

The Derbyshire Courier 26th August 1916
HASLAND'S FURTHER LOSSES
AN UNFORTUNATE FAMILY

The Hasland family of Mellor have been extremely unfortunate in the losses they have sustained in the War. Three brothers reside in the village Messrs. James, Jabez, and Joseph and during 1915 each of them lost his eldest son. Private Ernest Mellor Scots Guards son of James died of typhus whilst a P.O.W. in Germany; in February Private Wilfred Mellor of the Notts and Derbys Regiment son of Jabez was killed in

France on 6th March; Private Willoughby Mellor of the Royal Marines son of Joseph who lives in York Street met a similar fate in the Dardanelles on 8th May. Whilst this week the latter has received news to the effect that his second son Private John Mellor of the Royal Fusileers has been killed in action in France. The intimation was conveyed in an official document from the Infantry Records Depot Hounslow which states that the young soldier met his fate on the 3rd August. Private John Mellor was 20 years of age and studying for the scholastic profession, was educated at the Hasland National School where he gained a scholarship tenable for four years at Chesterfield Grammar School and whilst there, was successful in obtaining a scholarship enabling him to study at Cheltenham College. The latter place had been taken over by the Military Authorities and he had to wait twelve months before he could enter Chester College. In the meantime he took a position of pupil teacher at St. Helen's Street School Chesterfield. Attesting under Lord Derbys. Group Scheme he was called up on 16th April and entered the Public Schools Battalion the 28th Royal Fusiliers. He trained at Edinburgh for only three months and was drafted to France on the 29th July. There he was transferred to another Battalion from which he went into the firing line.

The sympathy of Hasland residents is extended to Mr and Mrs Mellor in their second loss which is rendered more acute from the fact that the deceased never had a furlough and had not been seen by them since he donned the King's colours. He was a respected member of the Hasland Primitive Methodist Sunday School prior to entering college.

The Derbyshire Courier 9th September 1916
HASLAND SOLDIER KILLED

A few weeks ago Mrs Hollingworth of Hoole Street, Hasland and formerly of Winsick received news from France to the effect that her second son Private George Hollingworth (20) of the Lincolnshire Regiment was missing and much anxiety was felt as to his whereabouts. On Monday official notice was received from the Infantry Records Office, Lichfield that he was killed in action on 11th July. Private Hollingworth enlisted, together with a number of Hasland youths all members of the Brotherhood, in the Lincolns in September 1914, and of these several have fallen, that is Privates Rawson, Pell, Rowland and Hopkinson whilst Corporal W. Needham and Private W. Cooper are prisoners-of-war in Germany, the last five meeting their fate at the Loos Battle in September 1915. Private Hollingworth was drafted to France five or six weeks after his companions he having an injured ankle when they went out. He was a prominent member of the Hasland Brotherhood Football Team and prior to enlistment was employed in the Black Shale Pit of the Grassmoor Colliery Company.

The Derbyshire Times 28th October 1916

Official news has been received from the War Office by Mrs J. Williams, Railway Terrace, Hasland, saying that her grandson Pte. Walter T. Williams (The Leics. Rgt.) has been killed in action. He enlisted on March 21st 1915 and on June 25th last was drafted to France. In civil life he was employed by the Grassmoor Co.Ltd.

Mrs Williams has had three sons in the Army. Wilfred who was killed in France a week ago. Bomb. J. Williams in hospital, he having had the misfortune to injure a foot, and the third is still in France.

The Derbyshire Times 24th February 1917
HASLAND MAN KILLED

Another of Hasland's young men has given his life for his country. This is Pte. Charles Cuthbert Hollingworth aged 29, fourth son of Mr William Hollingworth, The Green, Hasland. Pte. Hollingworth was well known and liked in the district and when at home last Easter told some of his many interesting and exciting experiences at the Front especially at Ypres and The Somme. He was always keenly interested in Motoring and was for a time at the Broad Oaks Motor Works. Just previous to

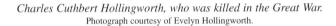

Charles Cuthbert Hollingworth, who was killed in the Great War.
Photograph courtesy of Evelyn Hollingworth.

joining the A.S.C. Mechanical Transport Section about a year ago, he was employed as a driver on the Chesterfield Corporation motor buses.

The first intimation that his father received was in a letter from one of Pte. Hollingworth's friends and this was to the effect that they were sleeping in a motor lorry on the night of February 9th when they were attacked by enemy aircraft and a shell burst about ten or twelve yards away. A fragment of this pierced the lorry and caught Hollingworth in the chest. On Monday an official intimation came to hand that he was dangerously wounded and was in No.2 General Hospital, Havre. This was followed by further official news on Wednesday night that death had ensued. On one occasion near Ypres, his car was blown up when he was in an adjoining dug-out

The Derbyshire Times 10th March 1917
HASLAND SOLDIER'S DEATH

We regret to record the death of Pte. A. F. Arnold, Sherwood Foresters who we reported in our last issue was so severely wounded by the bursting of a shell that his left leg had to be amputated. From the first Pte. Arnold's condition was very serious and it was recognised that he would have a struggle to pull through.

The third son of Mr and Mrs E. S. Arnold, Square & Compass, Chesterfield the deceased soldier leaves a widow and two children residing at Devonshire Avenue, Hasland.

Before enlisting in May 1916 he was employed in Chesterfield Corporation Tramway Department.

The Derbyshire Courier 24th March 1917
HASLAND SOLDIER KILLED
SHELL VICTIM

With the death in action of Private Albert Henry Kent (22) Machine Gun Corps sixth son of Mr and Mrs John Kent, Railway Terrace, Hasland only two of the gallant band of youths who enlisted together at the outbreak of War from the Midland Railway Cottages are now in the forces namely Privates E. Penn and W. Marriott, 2nd Corporal Tom Smith R.E.Military Medallist is working on munitions at Sheepbridge Works, and A. Wood is temporally discharged but the others have all made the supreme sacrifice.

The news of Private Kent's death was conveyed in a letter received by his parents last Thursday from Corporal F. Tomlinson. The deceased soldier was well respected in the district and was at one time in the choir of St. Augustine's Church, Derby Road. He joined the Sherwood Foresters on 2nd September 1914, went to France on 17th March 1915 and was afterwards transferred to the Machine Gun

Corps. He was wounded in May 1915 and on 17th July 1916 was buried for five hours. The writer of the above letter Corporal Tomlinson being awarded the D.C.M. for rescuing Private Kent and five other comrades.

Before enlistment Private Kent worked as assistant tuber at the Hasland Loco Sheds where his father is foreman fitter.

The Derbyshire Courier 24th March 1917
HASLAND SOLDIER KILLED
SHELL VICTIM

Mr and Mrs W. Pickering, Saunders Row, Hasland received news on Sunday of the death in action of their third son Private T. E. Pickering, Territorials, Sherwood Foresters. The intimation was made in a letter from Captain Victor Robinson. That there was a great affection between the deceased soldier and the late Lieutenant Jellicoe there can be no doubt for the same post brought a very sympathetic message from the latter's mother Mrs L. Jellicoe, of Earl's Court, London whilst hung in the front room of Mrs Pickering's house are enlarged photographs of the Private and his deceased Officer. Lieutenant F. W. A. Stubbs also conveys his sympathy and adds, 'He had been my servant since December he was most faithful, willing and trust-worthy. He was a splendid soldier and his record during the past two years is one of which you may be proud. He is buried amidst his fallen comrades and quite close to Mr Jellicoe.'

Private Pickering who was 24 years of age won a host of friends in civil life by his genial disposition and his loss will be keenly felt. He was one of the Old Territorials mobilised at the outbreak of War at Chesterfield and went to France in February 1915. He was previously employed in the Dunston (No 2) Pit of the Grassmoor Colliery Company.

The Derbyshire Courier 12th May 1917
UNFORTUNATE HASLAND FAMILY
SECOND SON KILLED

The Sympathy of all Hasland residents is this week extended to Mr and Mrs William Bradley, York Street in the loss they have suffered by the death in action in France of their second son Private William Bradley 20 years of age of the Dublin Fusiliers. Two years ago next Monday 14th May 1915 Private Bradley their eldest son died of wounds received in the Dardanelles at the age of 21 after only 6 months enlistment. These being the only two sons eligible for the Army it is hard for the parents to be bereft of both at such an early age. Official intimation of William's death was received from the War Office on Wednesday stating that he was killed in action on the 16th April. Private Bradley enlisted on 6th April 1916 and was passed for home service being attached to the Lincolnshire Regiment. Up to Last Christmas when he was at home on furlough he had been mostly engaged in his trade as a joiner erecting huts and various other jobs but just afterwards he was passed for active service. His training for a soldier did not commence until the early part of this year and he was drafted to France in March. Ten days before he was killed he was transferred to the Dublin Fusiliers.

The deceased soldier was a respected member of St. Paul's Church and was also connected with the Churchmen's Institute and the news of his death will be received with regret by a large circle of friends. Previous to enlistment he was in the employ of Messrs. J. H. & F. W. Green, Whittington Moor having commenced his apprenticeship with Mr S. Brailsford of Hady.

The Derbyshire Courier 16th June 1917
HASLAND SOLDIER'S DEATH FROM WOUNDS

Official intimation was received on Saturday from the Territorial Records Office, Lichfield by Mr and Mrs William Metcalf, Kent Street, Hasland that their fourth son Private Fred Metcalf, Sherwood Foresters, had died in the field from wounds in France on 15th May 1917. The parents had been anxious as to the safety of their son who was a consistent writer. They had received no communication from him for three weeks. Their fears were not lessened when they received a returned parcel which was marked 'wounded' the authorities being unable to trace him. The deceased who was 32 years of age enlisted in January 1915 went to France in October of the same year and was sent to Huddersfield Hospital in June 1916 suffering from illness. He returned to France in November 1916. Previous to joining the forces he worked for the Derbyshire County Council on the main roads in the Chesterfield District.

The Derbyshire Courier 4th August 1917
HASLAND SIGNALLER KILLED

Mr F. H. Day, Hampton Street, Hasland had only two sons. The elder Frank Ernest enlisted in the Leicestershire Regiment in March 1915 and was badly wounded in the head at The Battle of Loos in September the same year. After being in hospital for 12 months', during which time he underwent six operations, he was discharged. The younger, Signaller Albert Victor Day, enlisted in the Royal Garrison Artillery in October 1915, going to France on the 31st May 1916 and on Friday Mr Day received news that he had been killed in action. The first intimation was conveyed in a letter received from Sergeant John H. Gilmour, 94th Siege Battery, R.G.A. A further letter was received on Saturday from Gunner G. Houghton who had been the deceased s companion since training at Stockcross soon after enlistment. He stated that Signaller Day was doing duty on a night working party when he was struck, whilst official news was received from the War Office on Sunday stating that he was killed in action on the 10th July. The residents of the village extend their sympathy to Mr Day in his bereavement for the deceased soldier was much esteemed in the district where he had won a host of friends by his cheerful disposition. The loss of his mother a few years ago he felt keenly and often in private conversations amongst his comrades he referred in affectionate terms of his parents.

Previous to joining the Forces Signaller Day who was 24 years of age worked on the ovens of Hasland Coking Company where his father and brother are at present employed.

The Derbyshire Courier 22nd December 1917
AN ESCORT OF AEROPLANES
MILITARY FUNERAL OF A HASLAND SOLDIER

Bombardier Arthur Goodwin, Royal Field Artillery, third son of Mrs Goodwin of Kent Street, Hasland and of the late Mr Samuel Goodwin died on Wednesday of last week at Barnet War Hospital, Higher Barnet, Herts. from wounds received in France on the 8th October last. He was treated at Barnet but later was removed to the Ewen Hospital nearby 'for convalescence'. Whilst there, serious developments occurred and he was sent back to Barnet Hospital for treatment. It was found that septic poisoning had set in and his condition became critical. His mother was sent for on Tuesday 4th December and remained at Barnet until the end came as stated. The deceased soldier had expressed a wish to be buried at Barnet with full military honours and the interment took place on Saturday. The Commanding Officer of the district camp headed the cortege followed by a number of soldiers with arms reversed and the body was conveyed on a gun carriage drawn by four horses. Nearly five hundred wounded soldiers of Barnet and Ewen Hospitals followed as their last tribute of respect together with a number of the nursing staffs from both institutions and there was an escort of four aeroplanes. Soldiers with fixed bayonets formed the guard for the approach to the church. Three volleys were fired over the grave and the last post sounded.

The family mourners present were Mrs Goodwin (mother), Mrs Kerry (Leeds, sister), Mr Ernest Goodwin and Mr Harold Goodwin (brothers). Bombadier Goodwin's eldest brother Harry who is also serving with the Artillery in France was unable to attend.

The deceased who was 28 years of age was very popular in the village always cheerful and his death is deplored by a large circle of friends. He was a footballer of considerable repute and for several seasons assisted the Hasland Clubs at outside-left. He enlisted on 1st September 1914, went to France in May 1915, was wounded in the Somme Battle in September 1916, and returned to France in April this year. Previous to enlistment he worked in the Deep Hard (No.8) Pit of the

121

Grassmoor Colliery Company.

The Derbyshire Times 10th August 1918
CHESTERFIELD CASUALTIES

Mr and Mrs R. Lynn, York Street, Hasland have suffered a heavy loss by the death of their only son Private Cyril Lynn of the West Yorkshires joining originally the Yorkshire Light Infantry in August 1917 when 18 years of age. He was called suddenly to France about Easter this year following the German push of March 21st. Previous to enlisting Private Lynn was employed as a clerk at the Hotel Portland, Chesterfield. Before that he was for a time a clerk in the M.R. Goods Depot, Chesterfield. The official notification of his death in action on July 19th was received on August 1st. Thus Private Lynn was only 19years of age two days before he was killed.

The Derbyshire Times 9th November 1918
THE WAR
CHESTERFIELD CASUALTIES

Private Jabez Attenborough, Sherwoods formerly a greengrocer at Hasland and latterly a miner at Grassmoor Colliery died from influenza in Italy on October 30th. He leaves a widow and two children.

The Derbyshire Times Saturday10th January 1920
HASLAND GRASSMOOR BOND'S MAIN & DISTRICT

Much sympathy will be felt for Mr and Mrs W. Dumelow and family, Storforth Lane, Hasland in the loss of their son Charles who died on Saturday through illness contracted while a soldier. Deceased who joined the R.F.A. as a gunner in January 1915 was at the Dardanelles up to the evacuation, also in Egypt and Mesopotamia and then in Palestine up to the Armistice. He was demobilised in February last year but his health was undermined by his services in such hot countries. Previous to joining up he was at the Bond's Main Colliery and was a member of the Hasland Brotherhood and of the Hasland United F.C. and the Workingmen's Club.

SOLDIERS KILLED IN THE
SECOND WORLD WAR 1939-1945
WHOSE NAMES ARE ON THE HASLAND CENOTAPH

ADAMS - CHARLES
ALCOCK - SYDNEY
ASHMORE - FRANK
BLANKSBY - ALAN
BOWEN - FREDERICK
BROWN - JOHN
CARR - FRED
CHEESEWRIGHT - PETER
DAVISON - KENNETH
EDENBROW - BERNARD
GARNER - DAVID
HADLEY - WILLIAM
HIBBERT - ERIC
HIGGS - PERCY
JACQUES - JOHN
LORD - ALBERT
LOWE - FRANK
MARRIOTT - JACK
MOTHERSOLE - DENNIS
PLATER - DENNIS
PRESSWOOD - GEORGE
SHELBOURNE - WALTER
SIMMONDS - THOMAS
TAYLOR - CLIFFORD
VARDY - ROY
WALE - ALFRED
WATSON - IAN
WATTS - HARRY
WEBBER - JOHN
WILLIAMS - ARTHUR
WILLIAMS - GEORGE
WILSON - WILFRED

INFORMATION ON
THE DEATHS OF SOME OF THESE SOLDIERS

FRANK ARTHUR ASHMORE

Frank Arthur Ashmore was a Private in the Queen's Own Cameron Highlanders when he died at Dumfries Galloway Infirmary on 9th May 1945 aged 17 years. He was buried at Hasland Cemetery. He was the son of Alfred E. and Mary Ashmore of Hasland.

BERNARD EDENBROW
KILLED IN ACTION

Bernard Edenbrow was a Private in the Notts. and Derbys. Regiment of the Sherwood Foresters when he was killed on 4th September 1944.

Official notification was received this week that Pte. Bernard Edenbrow (29) whose wife lives at St. Augustine's Road, Chesterfield was killed in action on September 4th while serving with the Sherwood Foresters in the Central Mediterranean. He was the eldest son of Mr and Mrs H. Edenbrow, Talbot Street, Hasland, Chesterfield and before joining the army in the early part of the war was employed as a screen hand at Grassmoor Colliery. He had been abroad over two years, and served in the North African Campaign.

DAVID WILLIAM GARNER

David William Garner was a Sapper with the 615 Field Squadron Royal Engineers when he was killed on 6th March 1945 aged 32 years. He was the son of David and Sarah Jane Garner of Hasland and the husband of Myra Garner of Highfields, Leicester.

WILLIAM HADLEY

William Hadley was a Corporal in the Royal Marines on H.M.S. Warspite when he was killed on 23rd May 1941 aged 21 years. He was the son of Joseph and Martha Harriet Hadley of Hasland.

PERCY WILLIAM CHARLES HIGGS
PRESUMED DEAD

Percy William Charles Higgs was a Sergeant in the Royal Air Force when he was killed on 24th August 1943.

Mr and Mrs A. W. Higgs, North Terrace, Midland Cottages, Hasland, Chesterfield have received official information that their only son, Sgt. A.G.P.W.C. Higgs (22) who was posted missing from an operational flight on August 23rd is now presumed to have lost his life on that day. Before joining the R.A.F. four and a half years ago he was employed at the Loco Dept. L.M.S. Hasland. He was a pupil at Hasland Hall School.

FRANK LOWE

Frank Lowe was a driver with the Royal Army Service Corps when he died on 10th June 1944 aged 22 years. He was the son of Mrs A. G. Lowe of Hasland.

DENNIS LESLIE MOTHERSOLE

Dennis Leslie Mothersole was a Pilot Officer with the Royal Air Force Volunteer Reserves when he died at Oxford on 16th May 1945 aged 21 years. He was buried at Hasland Cemetery. He was the son of Wilfred and Mary Isabella Mothersole of Hasland.

The Derbyshire Times 7th March 1941
THOMAS HERBERT MELVIN SIMMONDS

Mr and Mrs T. Simmonds, 1, Smithfield Avenue, Hasland received official information last week that their son Sergeant Thomas H. M. Simmonds R.A.F. (wireless operator and air gunner) had been killed in action.

Sergeant Simmonds was 18 years of age and was educated at Tupton Hall Secondary School and joined the R.A.F. in February 1939 and passed through college and received full qualifications as a wireless operator. His father Mr. T. Simmonds saw much service during the last war and received the following decorations D.S.O., M.C., D.C.M. and was mentioned in despatches.

Thomas Herbert Melvin Simmonds was a Sergeant in the Royal Air Force when he was killed on 23rd February 1941.

ROY VARDY

Roy Vardy was a Guardsman in the Grenadier Guards when he died at King Edward 7th Hospital, Windsor on the 1st August 1945 aged 18 years. He was buried at Hasland Cemetery. He was the son of John and Lucy Vardy of Hasland.

IAN WATSON

Ian Watson was a Rifleman with the London Rifle Brigade when he died on 26th June 1944 aged 21 years. He was the son of Robert Bruce and Lucy Watson of Hasland.

HARRY WATTS

Harry Watts was a Private in the Notts. and Derbys. Regiment of the Sherwood Foresters when he died at the Military Hospital, St. Hugh's College, Oxford on 10th July 1940 aged 26 years. He was buried at Hasland Cemetery.

ARTHUR ASQUITH WILLIAMS

Arthur Asquith Williams was a signalman in the Royal Corps of Signals when he died on 25th December 1943 aged 18 years. He was buried in Hasland Cemetery. He was the son of Frank Daniel Asquith Williams and Mabel Alice Asquith Williams of Hasland.

GEORGE ASQUITH WILLIAMS

George Asquith Williams was a Private with the Duke of Wellington's West Riding Regiment when he died on 3rd February 1944 aged 26 years. He was the son of Frank Daniel Asquith Williams and Mabel Alice Asquith Williams. He was the husband of Hilda Williams of Boythorpe.

Hasland Drun Corps leading the Hasland Carnival procession.

The Play Chat float in the Hasland Carnival 1988.

The Play Chat float at the Hasland Carnival procession 1986.

The Play Chat float in the Hasland Carnival procession 1988.

MEMORIES

IDA BATES

I wondered what your earliest memory was?

My earliest memory, oh gosh that's not easy. Now I can always remember Easter time and it always used to be lovely and sunny, never rained (laughs) and my Uncle Will used to hide these Easter Eggs down in the orchard on Storforth Lane where they lived, and we all used to go finding them and I can always remember that and it was lovely.

Yes that's always stuck in my mind. Of course I can remember going from school, when I should be about seven, I always went straight up to Auntie Alice's to have some rice pudding. She made Uncle Will a rice pudding for him coming in from work and he used to save me some. That's another memory, yes that's another memory. I can always remember we'd got a copper in the corner that boiled clothes, and we used to have to have a fire underneath this copper boiling water and it was horrible, steamed up. That's another memory, that's not a very nice memory that isn't.

We used to have to go to chapel on Sunday night and sit in the family pew, very old fashioned. Then afterwards we went for a walk, and we used to go a horrible walk which was through the pit yard at Grassmoor. I used to hate it, all steam oozing out of places and I hated it. That's another memory (laughs). After going through this pit yard we used to go to some relations that lived at Grassmoor but we always had some fruit cake when we got there which was very nice. I enjoyed that.

Sometimes on a Sunday night we went down to my Auntie Ethel's house. They were related to my Mother and we always visited them. They lived on Derby Road and we walked it down Storforth Lane. Oh I used to hate that walking, and walking back up. Always had to go 'cos there was no television of course or anything like that, so of course we used to visit relations. My Dad always wore his bowler hat. Also, every Bank Holiday Monday, my Dad used to take us on that Light Railway to Ashover and I can remember going up Derby Road. I don't know where we got on it 'cos we used to walk up Derby Road to get on it. It was a little Light Railway that ran us to Ashover. That was lovely I used to think that was great. We did used to walk over the Golf Links as well. I can remember that but I used to hate that, going back up Storforth Lane. Oh that trail it seemed a trail. Down Langer Lane it's a long way when you're small. We used to go to Eastwood Park every night playing as well, but I mean there is nothing significant about it. But we used to go and play in the park for hours. Course you could in those days, you could then. But now you wouldn't dare let children play there on their own. Oh yes we were free weren't we, very free. We used to play down our garden a lot 'cos we'd got a big garden. Yes and you see we'd got that big shed, I can remember we used to play at shop in that shed because we d got all these big kind of tubs with wheat and Indian corn in all of them. Yes, I can remember that. It was a lovely big garden down there. So I think we spent a lot of time really in the garden playing. My Dad and Uncle Will bought a field between 'em. I mean in them days it was a big thing to do. Then they built the houses you see, The Elms and The Cedars. Yes I can remember them being built. I can remember flitting but I don't know what age I'd be. It was somebody called Ellis built them, funny that I can remember that. Our house was built first and we'd got all that garden. I can remember at bonfire night what a good night we used to have. Auntie Alice and all of them all banded together, and my cousin Hilda was good, she used to make a big Guy Fawkes. They all used to make bonfire toffee as well. It used to be a lovely night 'cos we'd room to have a bonfire, lovely bonfire and all things. Whenever we had parties, we always had both houses, all that room you see, they weren't separated as such because we'd always got a path that led from one house to the other. I was always at Auntie Alice's, I used to nearly live there. I think they had me to live there when I was a baby after my Mother died. That's why I should cling to 'em you see. They really spoiled me. Oh aye, Auntie Alice meant a lot to me, it was a big thing to me when she died. Yes they were ever so good to me, they all were, so I were very lucky actually. I mean I were more lucky than my sister Nellie in a way, because she were that bit older when our Mother died. It'd be worse for the older ones. My cousin Edna Wheeldon, she used to remember things about me being a baby after my Mother had died, because she lived next door to Auntie Alice when she lived on York Street. She said they used to wheel me about in a doll's pram (laughs) and she says I used to cry and cry and cry and she said her mother used to say if this baby lives we shall never give up on anybody else anymore, and I've lived longer than any of them. (laughs). I think I was a struggle to 'em but they did it all between them didn't they, so as I say, I had an unfortunate start but I'm having a good finish aren't I?

I went to Eyre Street School to start with. I can always remember having May Day and we always had to vote for a May Queen but it was never me (laughs) and I loved it because we had a maypole and took flowers. That was lovely, we danced with these flowers round the maypole that was a lovely memory. Another nice memory was because my cousin Eva was a teacher there when I was at that school, I thought I was big stuff, because I could go and see Eva if I wanted to. I can always remember when we went up to the school on The Green and we used to have a skipping rope which reached from one side of the road to the other, and we could skip all the way up Storforth Lane. This skipping rope stretched across the road, so there were no buses no traffic which you couldn't do now. I can remember doing that ever so plain. I can just remember that we had Mr Boden for the headmaster at the Green School and he was very, very strict and horrible, and they used to have a school choir. To pick the singers he used to walk into a schoolroom and just point at a person and say 'Sing this note' and he asked me and I opened my mouth and nothing came out 'cos I was too nervous (laughs). That's a bad memory, I can always remember that.

We went to the Methodist Church Sunday School when it was on Chapel Street, when there were all those rooms upstairs, it was lovely. I can remember when we used to have the Bazaar, Church Bazaar and it used to last for three days, and the building used to be full. Oh it was a great event that was. I always remember they served, we thought it was lovely, jelly, two colours of jelly on a plate you could have (laughs) what a treat. Oh, and Sunday School anniversaries, they were gorgeous, yes. Two Sundays mornings afternoons and evenings and the Church used to be full, they even had chairs down both aisles and the children on a big platform. We all had to have a new dress and new shoes. There was an Action Hymn, – I liked the Action Hymn, I loved it. On ordinary Sundays Vera Stevenson and I were in the choir, and we had the honour of putting the numbers up for the hymns, that was a big honour. About all we could happen manage between us (laughs). They were good days. All our social life was to do with Sunday School. They used to have social evenings, and we used to have a Concert Party which Vera and I were in. Mary Needham was a good pianist and she got this Concert Party up and we used to do a concert and a panto at Christmas, it was lovely. My cousin Kathleen was in it as well, we were called the Scarlet Revellers. There was a Committee which was Eric Norman and Fred Holleworth. They used to sit there and see if it was fit to do for the public, and your public was your mother and father and your cousins and your aunties and your grandmas (laughs). Yes it was lovely, we had a good social life.

When we went on holiday we went to Blackpool but we always had to go to stay with a family called Barlow at Blackpool because they came from Hasland and went to Hasland Methodist Church. They left Chesterfield and went to Blackpool and took a boarding house. So we had to go to there, and that's about all we did, went to Blackpool. I went to Cleethorpes once with Uncle Will, Auntie Alice and my cousin Doris. I also used to go to Morecambe with my brother Harry and his wife Lucy, he was my eldest brother and he was a lot older that me. They used to always take me and Lucy s sister as a pal for me. Harry and Lucy went to live in Canada. When I met Arnold and we used to go for a weekend to Blackpool they'd only allow us to go together on condition that we went to Barlows. Methodist people from Hasland you see, to keep an eye on us (laughs).

I can remember some of the shops in Hasland, oh yes. Opposite where the Co-op is now was Normans which sold wheat and corn and they used to deliver at our house on Storforth Lane. In fact they lived next door to us when we lived in Eyre

Street before they moved to the shop, that's right, and they had a baby and he died of meningitis. I can remember that so plain it was such a sad thing. I can remember Coppings, everybody will remember Coppings shop. Mr Copping, Walter Copping, I can remember him going round on a push-bike delivering papers, shouting Green-un. Yes, I bet, everybody, all old Hasland folk can remember them. There was Miss Cope next door to Coppings, lovely little shop that. Every Saturday night Arnold and I, we used to go in and buy cream buns and go back and eat 'em at home (laughs). Oh yes, she used to sell those lovely cream puffs, beautiful. She used to make a big fuss, well she was a fussy person, she probably made a fuss of every-body but we thought she just made a fuss of us you see. There was Woodheads which now is Kate's Pantry I think. Then there were all like little shops. There was Wilbourne's chemist, that was there forever, all those years that was. They used to go and play tennis, Mr and Mrs Wilbourne, I can always remember that. There was Harold's shoe shop which was there for years and years. That was next to the chemist. I'll tell you whose shop I always used to think was all dingy and dark, Jack Hallam's hardware shop on Hampton Street. Oo yes, it was all fusty-ish like they are, I mean he sold them sort of things. Then there was Jacksons the bakers further along there, they were there for years. A bit further along there was a printers years ago, – years and years it was always a printers. The Post Office was on The Green, that was there for years and years and years and they were always Slinns. Then next to that was Darnells, before you get to those houses, it was Darnells fruit shop and fish, they used to sell fish as well.

I left school at 14, yes that's right. I went straight to work at a shoe shop in Town but I didn't stay long, I was too shy to be in a shop. After that I went into tailoring. Wrights Tailors in Town, it was next to where the Baby Linen Shop is now, opposite the Victoria Centre on Knifesmithgate. They're not there any more, well no tailors are there now. We used to work in a little room right at the top of this building and when it was very hot it was hot 'cos it was like in an attic and we used to sit with our feet in a box of buttons to keep cool (laughs). I used to walk to work going up Storforth Lane Terrace, over the field. At night when I came home I used to have to come back myself over that field when it was dark. Which you wouldn't ever dare do now. Then I started biking it to work, went on a bike but I wasn't very good at biking I used to just drop off for no reason (laughs). Anyway I managed to get to work on it. I worked there till I got married, and of course in those days we left work when we got married. I did go back. When they were busy I used to go back at Easter time just for a week or two.

We got married at the Methodist Chapel. We had the wedding reception at home at Storforth Lane and also used Auntie Alice's house as well, 'cos they were next door and we had two big rooms. I went and bought my wedding dress in my dinner hour, just on my own. Yes, to this shop in Glumangate. I think it was about £7.50 (laughs). We went away on the same day, we didn't have an evening do in those days. We went to Llandudno in the afternoon.

I thought it was a really nice place to live, Hasland, yes I liked Hasland, and we spent such a lot of time in the park. Even when we were older we still spent a lot of time at the tennis courts. We used to spend hours playing tennis, and then there was the bandstand. All I can remember is that the tennis courts were in the park off the path leading down to Hoole Street, that entrance. Yes, it was lovely growing up in Hasland.

MARY BODEN

What is your earliest memory?

I fell down when I was 2 years old and chopped the end of my nose off. My nose has had a flat end ever since!

Another early memory was when a doctor came to our house when my sister Margaret was born. It was 1920 and I was 3¹/₂ years old.

We had the usual toys that children had in the 1920's, dolls, doll's pram, skipping rope and a whip and top. We had a hoop, which we used to propel with a stick. We used to play hopscotch on the paving slabs in the street. I had a fairy cycle which I rode in the street, it was safe in those days as there was hardly any traffic. I also had a miniature shop with little bottles of sweets and a toy weighing scale. Also I had a blackboard and easel.

I attended Chapel Street School at age 5. Miss Armstrong and Miss Cooper were the teachers. Then I went to Eyre Street School where my teacher was Miss Lowe. Miss Walton was Headmistress. My sister Muriel was May Queen at Eyre Street School in 1920 or 1921. A Maurice Bagnall was the May King. I went from there to Hasland Green School. While I was there, I had to go to my Father Walter Copping's paper shop at playtime on Doctor's instructions, to have a glass of milk, as I had a calcium deficiency. This was before the days of school milk. The teachers were Miss Nellie Rowe, Mr Cooper and Mr Ted Simmonds. Both Mr Cooper and Mr Simmonds, quite late in their careers, taught my son Garry at William Rhodes School in the 1950's. Miss Marjorie Wadsworth, Miss Fox and Miss Heath were the other teachers. The Headmaster was Mr Boden (no relation) a strict disciplinarian. He lived in the house attached to the school and had a son Vivian and daughter Kathleen. Vivian became Lord Vivian Boden, one of the country's leading academics.

I left school at 14 years of age and worked at my Father's shop, as did my two sisters, although Muriel worked at John Turners for a spell.

When we were at Eyre Street School we had Christmas Puddings. We all took some ingredients to make them and Mrs Lowe cooked them. We also had little gifts. One year I had a dictionary, I still have it. We used to have a pillowcase for our Christmas Stocking and always did well for toys! We had an orange, apple and nuts, a treat in those days. One Christmas I had a chocolate 'Pip, Squeak and Wilfred' which was a strip cartoon in the Daily Mirror.

On May Day we had a Maypole in the school yard and used to sing a song 'Welcome, Welcome, Sweet May Day'.

At Easter we had a chocolate Easter Egg and we also had what was left at the shop! We decorated hard-boiled eggs. Some people used to roll these down a grass field, but we never did.

We used to play in the park, and we used to watch the Hasland Silver Prize Band and other bands, play on the bandstand there. My Father and his brothers played football for Hasland. Their cousin Wilf Copping played for Arsenal and England, but he never lived in Hasland. My Father presented a football trophy to Hasland Hall School to be played for annually.

When we were young we used to go to Blackpool each year and stay in a small hotel on The Promenade. We usually went by bus, but on one occasion we went in someone's car. During the school holidays I used to spend most of the time at my grandparents (Needham) pub, the Cutthorpe Hotel, now the Jolly Lads, or something like that. In my late teens I also went to Bournemouth with my Mother, sister and my cousin Eileen.

I can remember the twopenny rush at Hasland Pictures on Saturday mornings.

We once had a dog called Timmy which came from a circus at the Hippodrome in Town, also Dad kept pigeons in a loft at the top of the garden. One time they were sent to Doll in France. One got lost, but turned up two years later.

We always lived on York Street, my aunt and uncle lived next door. My Grandfather Needham had the two built when York Street was constructed towards the end of the nineteenth century. It was a strange layout upstairs with a small bedroom off the back bedroom. When we were young we had a live in maid, Annie Shawcroft, who came to us from Cutthorpe, as my Mother and Father worked full time in their newspaper shop. When I was 12 or 13, in about 1929, we had a bathroom installed off the kitchen, in what was the outside toilet and the coalhouse. Mr Marriott, Eddie Marriott's father, was the contractor and Dennis Haywood put the electrics in. Dennis Haywood had, a few years earlier, installed the electric supply, replacing the gas mantles. One switch in the hallway was wired upside down and it remained that way until my Mother died in 1985. It's probably the same now! Along with the bathroom we had a tiled fireplace installed in the living room at the same time, replacing the black lead range with side oven. In the living room there was a cupboard, floor to ceiling, which we used to store crockery, cleaning materials etc., a sideboard, table and chairs, a settee, a wooden armchair, and later a large wooden wireless. A bit cluttered really! Off the living room and under the stairs, down three steps was a pantry with stone slab shelves. The front room, although furnished, was rarely used, we had a settee in there and a piano, bureau and bookcase. There was a carpet square and the floorboards surrounding this were darkened. The tiled fireplace had a wooden surround, as did the hearth. The kitchen was basic with a cupboard, sink and a mangle. The floor was black and red quarry tiles. The two main bedrooms had fireplaces, but only occasionally were they lit, as they tended to be a bit smokey. Oakleys in Kent Street delivered our coal, just tipped up on the street, no bags in those days. You had to barrow it in yourself and swill the street down after! During the miner's strike in 1927 there was a soup kitchen organised in the Village Hall.

Originally, my Uncle Ernest Copping had a wooden hut, where he sold news-papers, on Hasland Toll Bar, near where the toilets are. I remember when I was young, delivering newspapers with him on the Railway Cottages and coming back via Park Hill, riding in the carrier on the front of the bike. When Uncle Ernest moved to Nottingham, my Father, who was a miner at Grassmoor Colliery, took over the hut. When it was planned to build the first toilets on the Toll Bar the hut was due to be demolished. Fortunately, there was an empty lock-up shop, owned by, and next door to Shentalls, on the opposite side of the road. It used to be a sweet shop, a Mrs White used to serve in it. My Father rented this shop and ran it as a newsagent, confectionary and tobacco shop for over 40 years. I used to cycle up to Grassmoor Station to pick up the 'Early Bird' racing papers from the train when I was 14 or 15 years old, and freewheel all the way back down Mansfield Road. After my Father's death in 1960 the business was acquired by his grandson, who ran it under the Coppings' name for a further 35 years.

I attended the Methodist Church and Sunday School when I was young, but at 12 years old I started attending St. Paul's Church. Although not a regular attender, I got married there in 1940. The officiating vicar was Rev. W. Vivian Davies M.A. Hilda Cheetham and Doug Lee, who kept the chip shop at the top of Hasland, got married there the same day. The Rev. Davies christened my son Garry in 1945.

The farms in Hasland that I remember were Heathcotes, up The Green, Manny Taylors opposite, and Tommy Lowe's farm next to Hasland Park.

I can remember some of the shops as well. There was Miss Cope's shop on Hasland Green which was owned by her Father and they lived at the rear of the shop. Strangely, Mr Cope was also manager of Woodheads across the road at the same time. Mr Gillings had a barber's shop next door to Miss Cope's and years later it was Evelyn Brown's ladies hairdressers. Frank Darnell had a greengrocer s shop on The Green. They later sold out to the Co-op. Mrs Darnell looked after the shop and Frank sold fruit and veg. from a horse and cart. Later Mr Vaines had a horse-drawn fruit and veg. cart. Miss Sedgwick, later Mrs Bunting, who had the shop at the corner of York Street and The Green, originally had a clothes shop in the premises opposite, which later was to become Jack Carr's Cobblers. In the block where Coppings, Shentalls and Chambers were, upstairs there was a Billiard Hall. Chamber s shop, which moved there from the block above the Devonshire Arms, was originally Norman's butchers. His brother had a butcher's shop in Calow Lane. Percy Norman had a butcher's shop on the Eyre Street/Hasland Road corner. They went to live in Southwold, Suffolk in the 1930's. I went to stay for a few days with them there, as I was friends with their daughter. Gothards had a butcher's shop at the York Street/Eyre Street corner and Fred Fearn had a butcher's shop on the corner of York

Street/Hampton Street. The China Shop on the opposite corner was the Indian and China Grocery Shop. A Mr Brown from Kent Street used to be the manager. The general shop opposite our house in York Street, about halfway down, was owned by a Mr Micklewright, then a Mr Waring. Later Bert Plater ran it and then Bill Ford, who was a member of a pools winning syndicate. Then Maurice De Ville. Garry delivered bread and groceries for both Bill and Maurice on one of those delivery bikes with a pannier and a small wheel at the front. Jackson's bakery on Hampton Street, used to be Allens Bakers run by a man and his sister. Next door to Wilbourne's Chemist on the front, Dora Harold had a shoe shop. There was another newsagent on Mansfield Road it was Laits, and later it was Barkers and then Brian Beeton kept it. Also on Mansfield Road there was a clothes shop run by Mr and Mrs Neal. Redferns had a butcher's in the premises later occupied by Keith Witham. Further up Mansfield Road, Annie Norman and her son Godfrey ran a shop selling corn in one half, and fruit and flowers in the other. Ethel Painter had a chip shop in York Street which was later Millwards and there were two others on Mansfield Road, Drivers, run by Hilda and Doug Lee, and Sharpes further down. These were all at one time, coal-fired. Dr Moyers was the local doctor. He lived and had a surgery at the top of York Street. Bradleys in York Street which was later run by Alf Cox, sold flowers and wreaths. I also remember Major and Mrs Lamenby who lived at Herne House up Mansfield Road, opposite Grassmoor Station. They opened all the social functions, bazaars, etc. Then there were Pecks who lived at Penmore House.

When the Second World War started in 1939 I was 22 years old. The German planes started coming over to bomb Sheffield. We didn't have an air raid shelter so we used to go into the pantry under the stairs. We had black-out curtains up to the windows. Some people had to go on Fire Watch and the A.R.P. were based upstairs at the Devonshire Arms. Food and sweets were rationed and we hardly had any fruit during the War years. We also had coupons for our clothing. I remember Sheffield being bombed early in the War on 12th and 16th December. No bombs, as far as I am aware, fell on Hasland, but one fell near Storforth Lane bridge. My husband Horace was once coming home on a 48 hour leave during the War, by train. The train didn't stop at Chesterfield and so he had to get off at Sheffield and get a local train back to Chesterfield. However, due to a bombing raid the train came to a standstill. Due to the black-out he wasn't sure where he was, except that he was over a bridge. When the train started moving again, he saw in the gloom the Crooked Spire! It appears that he was stuck over Storforth Lane bridge for 40 minutes! He wasted 6 hours of his leave getting back from Sheffield. In 1940 after the evacuation of Dunkirk some troops were due to be billeted near Hasland and were going down the streets looking for people to take them in and give them beds and lodgings. My Mother and Father took two soldiers in for a few days until a camp could be organised. One of the soldiers corresponded with my sister Margaret. After staying a while in and around Chesterfield the unit went to Northern Ireland and then to North Africa.. My sister didn't see Doug for almost four years. Then he came on leave, at that time he was then a Captain. They married by special licence and have been married almost 60 years and are living in Welwyn Garden City. Because of the war, people were living in rented accommodation, rooms, or like my husband and me, with parents or relatives.

Years ago everyone used to know everyone else in Hasland. As a village it was pretty well self-contained. Most people appeared to work at the 'Pit' or on the 'Railway'. We seemed to have all the tradesmen we needed in the village. Builders, electricians, plumbers, coalmen, chimney sweeps, garages and pubs. Sam Bell and Mr Parker had taxis. Very few people had cars in those days, people used to walk a lot, and there were buses, they had horse-drawn buses out in the sticks.

PEGGY GOODGE

I think my earliest memory was of starting at Sunday School or day school which at that time was on Chapel Street, the Sunday School, it was day school as well there, I can remember going there, I think that was the earliest thing I can remember.

I've lived in Hasland all my life. I was born up at Town End View, that row of houses up Mansfield Road just past the garage. I can't be sure whether my Mother was in lodgings before we got that house. I know they were in lodgings for a while and I think they then moved there. By the time I was born they were living in Hasland. I went to the Sunday Schoolrooms as school and Sunday School, Mrs Dean, I think was the teacher at day school. That was on Chapel Street. Then I moved to Eyre Street, then the Green, and then I was one of the first pupils at Hasland Hall. I was there on the day it opened, so I can remember that bit. I can't remember much about Eyre Street School but I can remember being with the May Queen there, as an attendant, I think it was Peggy Waring and myself who were attendants to the May Queen (laughs). I can't remember doing anything at the Green School of an outstanding nature, I've always been just in the backwaters (laughs). I do remember Hasland Hall. I remember the opening day and we had the people there whose names had been used for the different houses. I was in Middleton house and somebody from the Middleton family came, and there was a house called Lucas and there'd be one of the Lucas family, there was one of the Markhams too but I am afraid that is about all I can remember of that.

I cannot remember whether or not I had many toys. You know your parents were poor in those days and really your toys were very minimal, I don't remember having any specials. I'm sure I had a doll, not like they have now, but I can't remember having much. I mean, when we were up there, at Town End View, there was nothing in the front room. In fact, Miss Sedgewick who had a shop on the corner of York Street and The Green, well she started her business in my Mother's front room. She worked at Shentalls and she used to go round house to house with a suitcase, but she'd got all the clothes, her stock you know, in my Mother's front room, then she started the shop later on. She didn't go straight away there, I think she was on the front where all the shops are now, and then she moved to that corner. Then they went to live at Falmouth when she retired, and when my Father died she invited my Mother and I down to Falmouth, yes I remember that. Her married name was Bunting.

We celebrated Christmas, not wildly, but we all went to my Grandma's at Alfreton all the family. Yes, we had our pillowcases, we had good Christmases. Then as my Grandma got older they came to us when we lived up Mansfield Road, the family used to come to us. I can remember even though we were poor my Mother always made sure we had a good Christmas. Course in those days they used to pay all year into a Christmas Club, you know to buy the pork pies and everything. I can remember, we used to have for breakfast, pork pies brought out with the ham. Well it s a funny thing to have at breakfast-time isn't it? I think it might have been a tradition, yes I think it was. We enjoyed Christmas.

We had Easter Eggs, but I won t say a lot. I think we celebrated Easter because Easter was a big celebration at Church as well, you see. We went to the Methodist Chapel and there was always something going off at Easter there.

I can remember a few of the shops, I'm just trying to think what they were. You can't forget Wilbournes the chemist, everybody knows that. Mckays were at the first shop, they had two parts to the shop, mens and ladies. I don't know what was after them. I remember Miss Cope on the corner and Jacksons were on Hampton Street. There were a lot of butcher's shops. Yes there was Tom Lowes on the corner that was our butchers, and Mr Barnes on Hampton Street which is now the carpet shop. There were others as well. Fearns was at the top of York Street before Barnes. They went down south and opened a hotel, I can remember going to see them once when we were down there. I'm afraid I can't remember the other shops very well. I'm not a very observant person.

I was no more than fifteen when I left school, I would think. I got a job at the Tube Works and they sent me to a Calculating School (Comptometer School) for three months. Yes, I only stayed at the school a month because there was an outbreak of flu and they sent for me to come back to the Tube Works. I don't know how long you were supposed to do, three months perhaps, I had a month and they sent for me to come in and I never got back. Mind you it was hard work at Comp School, if you didn't get to division by the end of the first week you were out no matter if you could afford it or not. Yes, I did that, but I was a secretary more than doing that. I stayed at the Tube Works the whole of my working life. I retired at fifty-eight I think, took early retirement. I've no regrets really. In those days there weren't the jobs to keep moving on to. Now they've got to move on to get the experience, you can't just stop in one job. In my day if you liked it and the pay eventually was good, you stayed.

I can remember the War. Well I can remember the rationing when we only had so much butter, and so much tea and so much of everything else. In the butchers you only got a small piece of meat. The darkness, I can remember very well, cos they took all the street lights, they took the railings as well in front of your house, I remember that. They took those for the War effort. I can remember falling over our front wall. I was coming home one night and I thought I'd got to the entry to go in, and I fell over the wall into the garden (laughs). Someone shouted 'Are you alright?' and I said 'Yes thank you'. I didn't tell them what I'd done, I just scrambled up and went in. There were some good times as well as the bad. Because with being at the Tube Works, I was in a reserved job so I didn't have to go.

We moved from Town End View to here in 1954 and there was my Mother and myself then. I didn't get married till I was forty-five I think, it'd be about 1966 or something like that. There were three of us for a while and then there were still three of us when my husband joined us here, and we had my Mother with us. She lived till she was ninety. They both died in a week you know, Herbert and my Mother, which was a bit traumatic, but one gets over these things, you do in time.

My Father had never had a holiday you know, till he went with my Mother, they'd never been able to afford one. But we did, we used to go on holiday if it was only to stay with friends. We had friends outside Blackpool, we went there quite a bit. Oh yes we had a holiday, we didn't go abroad of course, now everybody goes. We had good holidays but never expensive ones. I can remember in some places you used to buy your own food and bring it in and it was cooked by the lady of the house. That was one of my earliest memories of a holiday, before you went up the scale and went to a boarding house and then to a hotel, if you were lucky.

I was never a very out-going person but I enjoyed the dances at The Victoria Ballroom in Chesterfield, they were alright. We had a nice little group of friends that used to go round with one another. But of course in wartime we were restricted quite a bit for going out because of the dark but I think we had a good time. We had little house group things, then of course I helped with a lot of things at chapel like they used to. Right from being big enough to go, I should think from four years old I went to the Methodist Church Sunday School. Talking about friends and social life, I was more of an introvert than an extrovert, if that's how they put it. But I'd got lots of friends there. I remember some of the teachers at Sunday School. There was Freda Stevenson, I can remember her, she lived at the end of Eyre Street. Her family were big people at our Church. Rachael Burton was, too. I think there were about seven teachers, oh yes, there was a Mr Baldwin and Miss Hancock another elderly lady, who lived down Calow Lane. I can remember her very well, she was quite a good age. Of course Kathleen Slatcher was a teacher when I first went and later on I was a teacher and she was still there (laughs). Mr and Mrs Slatcher gave their lives to that church. Well then next thing I knew I was helping with the Youth Club, that has quite a lot of memories, going to watch the lads play football, but I was older than the people in the Youth Club there. I should think five or six years. We took them to Darley Dale, there was a building there that you could rent and we took them there. I can remember Mr and Mrs Slatcher went too. We had some lovely times. Mr McCourt took the Drama Group, I think he was a paid teacher and I think he was classed as like a night school. Oh the plays were wonderful. I mean I was prompter at nearly all the plays, never in one, I would never be in one, but I did prompt. They were happy days. I think most of my memories are in that area to do with the church, but I never left, I mean I just graduated from being in the School myself to becoming a Sunday School teacher. I was in the choir too. I was class leader, you know, I had so many on my pastoral list to go and visit, I've only just come off that. Then I was communion steward for a long time as well. My Mother was involved with the Church before me, she'd done all the things, I sort of followed on. She was communion steward and I took over from her, yes, she was in the choir as well. My Father came to all the special things at Church but he didn't take part.

I always thought that Hasland was exceptionally good because it was a village then, there was not the hustle and bustle that there is in Hasland now. I mean it's no longer a village, it's joined up with Chesterfield now. Oh yes, it was a village and it was quiet, it was a very nice place I thought. There was the park and not many people had a nice park in those days. There were the recreations there, bowls and tennis. Yes I thought Hasland was exceptionally nice. But now the cars are just going past all the time, you can't call it a village. I mean they never used to have cars parking on Hasland Not like now, there were hardly any cars. My Father never had a car and it wasn't till I was married that we had a car. There were very few weren't there, only the well-to-do had cars.

JEAN HAZELL

What's your earliest memory?

I don't know. I always thought I could remember Grassmoor Pit Disaster but I can't tell you what year it was. Might have been '35, praps be before then. But they used to come down shouting with the papers and anybody running down the street shouting like that always sort of made me feel insecure. I always thought that was from the disaster. Apparently my Mother didn't know whether my Grandad was at work or not. It was his seam actually, and she must have bundled me up and we ran down to my Grandma's you see. Cos I was living at Storforth Lane at that time and it wouldn't be that far away. Another early memory is that I can remember sitting on the stairs at that house, 'cos I used to put my animals up on the steps and teach 'em (laughs). It was just like a square at the bottom of the stairs and I used to play there, I can remember that.

I had a teddy bear, I'd never have parted with him you know (laughs), but my Mother burnt him because she said he was moth-eaten. I had a large dog 'cos Dad had a dog. I don't think my Mother was very keen on dogs (laughs) so I didn't get a real dog. But I had quite a large toy dog that was sat up. I called him Vic, I can remember him. I had more animals than dolls I think. I had a doll with a pot head and a sort of a stuffed body. I've got a photo of me sat on a swing with a rabbit or something with big ears stuck up, I can remember that one.

My Dad used to take us sometimes Sunday evenings to Town to the bandstand there where they had brass band concerts. There was a bandstand in Hasland Park as well. I can remember the two bowling greens in the park, cos my Dad played bowls. He sometimes used to take me up there, and there was like an old wooden tram that over-looked one of the bowling greens and I used to play in there.

They did tell me that they took me on holiday to Cleethorpes for the first time and lost me (laughs). There's this little boy statue with a leaking wellington boot, it drips out of the heel or somewhere and that's where they found me looking at that. So hard luck they got me back! (laughs). Then after that they went to Blackpool, and of course my Grandma and Grandad went and sometimes my Aunt Doris. We always used to go to the show on the south pier and the fol-de-rols and Harry Corris was the main comic. During the War they used to have a show on the wireless, there was Harry Corris, somebody and me. There were three of 'em and they used to act about and sing funny songs and things like that. I can't remember what it was called but it was on the wireless on Sunday evening so we weren't allowed to have it on. That always bugged me (laughs) 'cos they talked about it at school I suppose. I can remember the programme called ITMA, but that must have been on in the week, we never missed ITMA with Tommy Handley.

I can't remember starting school but I went to Eyre Street School. You didn't have to go to school till you were five but you could go at four. I went at four but my cousin Howard didn't, cos my Uncle Horace said 'They re at school long enough' (laughs) So Howard didn' t come till he was five. We used to have like rush mats or cords, they were sort of oval. We used to put em all on the floor and lie down and have a nap in the afternoon. I can remember that. I can't remember that lady's name, but we all liked her. Miss Cooper taught the top class. You see you don't know how old your teachers are do you, they always look old (laughs) and they weren' t some of them. She was a plump lady, and one day something had upset me at school, and she'd had me sat on her knee. I went home and I was telling my Mother about whatever it was, and I said to my Mother 'Miss Cooper's knee's more comfortable than yours' (laughs).

One day, Howard and I were coming out from Eyre Street School and our Aunt Mabel who lived a few doors away from the school, was stood in her front window watching us come out. We must have been quite near 'cos she heard what we were saying. These boys were coming and they used to chase us and I said 'Come on Howie let's run' and he gave me his cap and says 'Naiw, let's fait 'm' (laughs). Aunt Mabel told 'em that story of course, I can't remember it actually.

I went to the Green School from there, and I must have been at that school when my Father died, 'cos we went up there at seven. It was laid out, with two classrooms at the front and one room at the back. I think I started in the room at the back, but I can't remember the teacher. Then I went across to the one at the front, which was at that end. There was me and one other girl and we were always getting into trouble for our writing, because we were doing real writing by then. The teacher was always grumbling at we two about our writing. Turog, that was bread you know, they did a competition. It was all the schools in Town as far as I know. Well this girl and myself we won a prize for our writing. So I think that shut her up (laughs). The Headmaster was Mr Keeton I think, I don't think they had a headmistress. Then we went into the other room at the front and it was Mr Pearson, that was the next to the top class and we all thought he was marvellous. At the end of that year he left and went to Tapton, and I immediately wanted to go to Tapton (laughs). The only thing was when I got to Tapton the first time I saw him he walked straight past me and completely ignored me. I'm quite sure he couldn't have forgotten someone from his class that he had taught all the time. It was only a year before (laughs). So I went off him (laughs). Oh and Miss Pickard, she took the top class. I think we must have been being noisy because she said 'The next of you that start talking will be out at the front for the cane'. I was one of 'em! That s why I've always been repressed (laughs). When they say they shouldn' t give you the cane because it upsets you, well I don't think it hurt me that much, it might have done at the time though (laughs). When you think about it, she must have got hundreds of children through that 11-plus, there were seventeen of us passed that year that I took the exam. For all three schools that is, but I mean that must have been nearly half the class.

In 1937 it was the Coronation and for some reason we were at school, I don't know whether we were having a party at school and they had windows which were called hoppers, that sort of came out and you could lift a pane out. It was pouring with rain and when anybody wanted to go to the toilet, which was across the yard, they were pushing them out through the window. We also had games up on Heathcote's Farm. There were mothers helping, 'cos my Mother was there. We had a tea and we had sports and everybody won something. If you weren't first, second or third you had to run again with all the others who weren't first, second or third and by the time you'd done everybody came either first second or third (laughs). I didn't realise that at the time though. We used to have egg and spoon races and all sorts of things like that. That's where my Mother said she saw this big old-fashioned fireplace and I'm not saying it was a Yorkshire range because I don't know, but it was as big as a Yorkshire range in the farm, the Manor House. There was a map over the fireplace, and I don't know who it was, whether it was Mr Heathcote pointed it out to my Mother. I don't know whether monks had lived at the Manor House, but he said that they walked down those fields, which you could do, and came out up that jitty onto Storforth Lane. Then crossed the road and went up the path over the fields. There was a path that s up the front of Storforth Lane Terrace, they walked across there, and across the other farm and on St. Leonard's Drive. There was Spital House, yes, they used to walk to that, so it must be a very ancient walk. My Mother was quite intrigued, she didn t know about it.

I'm never awfully sure how old I was when I went to senior school. I was in Miss

Pickard's class, I think it must have been when War broke out. We were going to go to Rhyl on a holiday from school and we couldn't go 'cos of The War. I never forgave Hitler for that (laughs).

I've got lots of memories of Tapton House, I mean, I was just happy all the time at school, particularly at Tapton, yes. I can't remember disliking school at all but Tapton was special, I always thought. All the people you meet who went there always seem to think the same, well, that I've met anyway. To me, it still belongs to me, Tapton does. I was talking to a boy recently and he was telling me he'd moved up there. He was telling me it belongs to the University. I said 'I went to school at Tapton' and he said 'Oh it isn't a school now'. I thought 'It is to me' (laughs).

I finished at Tapton House in 1944, I'd be nearly fifteen. Actually, what I did was, I had scarlet fever and never went back to school (laughs). I started with scarlet fever on the first day of School Certificate. My Mother went up to see 'tubby', the headmaster, (laughs) Mr Mellors. They were on about me going for another year you see, but she'd already kept me at school an extra year because we left at fourteen really. I'd done an extra year to get my School Certificate. She'd also got me signed up to go to the Comptometer School at Sheffield. Mr Mellor didn't seem to think I'd remember things with having this big gap and starting again, which I agree with him actually (laughs). So I didn't actually go back to school. I can remember the day I left because I felt so ill that at lunchtime, I went and asked if I could go home. He kept me standing at the side of his desk while he went through my Latin homework. Well I thought I was reasonably good at Latin, that's why I put it down. Anyway, he just went through, and he says 'There's really only your name at the top of the sheet that I can give you any marks on for this' and I was nearly collapsing at the side of him. I think they let me go home on the bus on my own. I got my own back though. When they found out on the Monday that I'd got Scarlet Fever they had 'em all queuing up outside the cookery room to gargle. They had the doctor to see me, they must have had him Sunday morning 'cos he said it was Scarlet Fever and I'd have to go in the hospital. Well, my Grandma and Grandad were at Chapel. I don t know whether Grandad suspected that s what it might be. But my Mother was hoping that Grandma would be out of the way until I'd gone, but when they came back from chapel the ambulance was in the gateway at the side of the house. Grandma always walked with an umbrella, and she went for the ambulance driver with the umbrella and she says 'You're not taking our Jean anywhere' (laughs). He was only a little fella, he couldn't even carry me into the ambulance 'cos I was too big (laughs). They took me into Penmore Hospital, and they could only visit Sundays and talk to you through the window. I don't know whether my Mother had come an extra day, 'cos I was quite poorly when I went in apparently. I was sat up in bed looking through the window when my Mother came, I said 'You're not going to stop very long are you' (laughs). I think it nearly killed my Mother that (laughs). But I can remember feeling so awful and sitting up in bed talking was just an effort. I was about the oldest in the ward. There were two wards, girls were in one end and boys were in the other, and there were like all the facilities and everything in between for the nurses and things like that. I had swollen glands, I think, three times and they used to make this poultice, put it on a cloth, and I'd have it round my neck and tied at the top with the two ends like rabbit's ears (laughs). I was in there for about a month.

I went to Comptometer School after that, and when you went to Comp School in my day they guaranteed to get a job for you at the end of your course. Clay Cross Company rang up because they wanted somebody for their colliery wages office, as this young woman was leaving. Her boyfriend was coming home on embarkation leave and as soon as he got home they were getting married. But she didn't know exactly when he'd come. Anyway they arranged for me to go for an interview. Grandad insisted on coming with me, mind you I don't think I'd ever been to Clay Cross before. Grandad took me and we went to have this meeting. There were two brothers, they were both there, they were sort of management over the Company. Jackson's owned it, but they didn't do any interviewing. Grandad said something about he'd come with me because he wanted to see where I was going to work (laughs) that would have lost me the job these days (laughs). They gave me the job but they didn't want me until this girl knew when she would actually be leaving you see, so I did an extra month at Comp School. When I was at Clay Cross Company, we went to General Jackson's funeral and his wife's as well. We all fell in love with the grandson who was in the forces, the Army I think. The whole Company went to North Wingfield Church to the funeral when I was there. Then of course when they were nationalised they had to move us, so I was taken over by the Coal Board with the chairs and the desks and the comp (laughs). We went to Pilsley for about a year and I went there on the blue bus, the Midland General. It dropped me off at the bottom of the pit lane and it was a long walk uphill to the offices, and to the pit. It was quite muddy and it was like slurry, a bit like, you know, all coal dust in it. It splashed up the back of my stockings which were lisle and it took the colour out of 'em (laughs). You see, you don't get things like that these days (laughs). Then they moved us to Holmewood and they put us in this house. Not actually in Holmewood offices, it was this big house a bit farther on. I can't remember how long we were there, but eventually they moved us down to the offices of Holmewood Pit and we had two rooms in there. Bond's Main was my pit when I started work at Clay Cross Company, I did all the comping for Bond's Main. When we got up to Holmewood, they closed Bonds Main because they took coal up through Williamthorpe. Most of the men went to Arkwright and we went with 'em you see. From Arkwright we went to Bolsover Schools that's where the Model Village is. When we went there, there were still two classrooms of children and we had two classrooms. I went to Markham from there. There was Arkwright, Markham which was three pits, Ireland, Area Workshops and the Estates Department. We did all their wages. There was a ballroom up there in the offices (laughs) I don't know why it was there, upstairs. We had that as our big room for the wages. They took us for one year up to the Area at Bolsover, I hated that. Then at the end of that year they decided they were goin to send us back out to the pit. Every pit'd actually have their own wages staff at the pit, and I think that was when they were starting on computerising.

At Christmas, when I was little, and my Dad was alive, we always went to Aunt Emma's for Christmas so I don't know what the rest of my Mother's family did. It was before the War of course. But I can remember Christmas at Aunt Emma's. It was quite a big house, she'd got a large dining room. It was at Ecclesfield. She lived on a hill, and it curved. She'd a bay window with a widish window sill and I could sit on that. They had these lamps and the lamplighter had to light 'em with his pole. He went down the hill and you could see one after another coming on round the corner. It was fantastic, I mean we'd got proper lights in Hasland and Chesterfield, very boring (laughs). I shared a bedroom with my Mum and Dad, and it was big, and it was cold, and the gas fire used to pop all the time. The brass band came round every Christmas morning playing carols. We could see Chapeltown from there and the Newton Chambers factory had got a chimney with a flare on and I thought it was great. It made my day when they had one down at the Carbonisation Plant (laughs). I thought 'I've got my own flare at last' (laughs). They made Izal toilet rolls, and for some reason or other they'd got nursery rhymes printed on 'em. I sat at Aunt Emma's in the toilet and pulled the roll right down to the end to read all the nursery rhymes (laughs). I did roll it back but I don't know what it'd be like by then. There was Aunt Emma, Aunt Ginny and Aunt Lizzie. Aunt Lizzie was a bit strange, but actually, in the First World War, she lost her husband and two sons within a fortnight, and it probably just tipped her over. I should think it'd be enough to. But of course, they used to have these pal's regiments, and they all came from the same place so they were all in it together you see.

I can remember in the Second World War, sitting under the stairs when the siren went because at first we hadn't got an air raid shelter. The sirens went off quite soon after the start of the War, probably on the first day or something like that and we sat under the stairs. We put a form in there and I don't know what else went in, stools praps, and we sat under there 'cos under the stairs was supposed to be one of the safest places in the house. I can remember, when we first got an air raid shelter, my Grandad put it down in the orchard and we used to trail down there when the sirens went, it were nearly a mile walk (laughs). Course you see it was sunk into the ground but there was so much above it, they covered that with soil or grass or something. Early on in the War there was a bomb dropped, you know where you go on Langer Lane and it dips down to the brook and you can go across a field. You could walk sort of on the bottom and then go up and come out against the Blue Stoops. We used to do that walk on Sundays when my Dad was alive. We always walked on Sundays in the Summer, my Mother, my Dad and me. Well, this bomb had been dropped on the bottom level piece. Grandad took me to have a look at it cos it was a great big hole (laughs) you couldn't see anything else it hadn't done anything else. They also dropped a bomb, you know when you come under the bridge, coming up Storforth Lane, there used to be a row of houses that came straight onto the pavement. A bomb dropped on the pavement and it blew the windows out. There was a family there that we knew, and it knocked him down behind the door and the door came in on top of him. There was nobody killed actually. Then there was one other bomb dropped near us. Across from my Grandma's there used to be a pit shaft in the field behind the builder's yard on Storforth Lane, it belonged to Grassmoor Pit. Well the bomb dropped in that field there and we were all in the front room. I don't think the sirens had gone that night. I was on my knees looking at something my Mother was reading, she was sat in the armchair, and I saw the curtains come in. I screamed and my Mother never heard the bomb cos all she heard was my scream in her ear (laughs). So those are our three bombs. I can remember seeing soldiers. They used to wear blue uniform when they were wounded. I don't know if that was always or whether that was just a hangover from the First World War. I can remember going to Town, course they always cleared the stalls in the market, and there were all these soldiers. They couldn't have been that injured but they were all in blue, and they were all sort of sprawled out on the floor in the market. Wherever they'd brought 'em from, they must have been moving 'em around the country you know to get 'em fitted in somewhere. Then there were the paratroops you know (laughs) at Holmewood. We had like 'Salute the Soldier' week, I can remember that 'cos we had little cardboard things, I don't know whether you had to buy 'em or what. They had speeches in front of the Town Hall and we marched to church, The Parish Church, and we went 'cos we were in the guides. There's two occasions I can remember. The paratroops were behind us, and it was hot and we guides were stood in front. Now the paratroops were falling rather like flies (laughs) but they had got all their kit on. We weren't, but I did. I can remember turning to my friend and saying 'I feel funny' and she caught me and the next thing I know I'd bumped into somebody (laughs). They took me somewhere but I went back into the parade, I wasn't that bad, but I had sort of fainted. There were only two women in the parade that fainted and I was one of them (laughs). The other incident about the parades which I remember. I'd got a flag for the Guide Company, and we definitely went to the Parish Church that time. All the flags went in together, and bearing in mind that I was chapel, I don't think at that stage I'd ever been anywhere else. All of a sudden this girl in front of me who was carrying a flag, she bobbed down in front of the altar, did like a curtsy, and I nearly fell over her (laughs). So whether she was Catholic or whether The Parish Church was high enough for 'em to do that I don't know, but I wasn't expecting anything like that (laughs). You remember things like that.

Of course I went to the Sunday School at the Methodist Chapel from being very small although I'm not sure how old I'd be. At the Anniversary we always did the action hymn. We were one long row, all girls, in the Action Hymn. We did it for years, and then after that I used to teach 'em the action hymn (laughs). It always seemed to be hot for the Anniversary, it was in May sometime. My Mother used to make me these white frocks with frills on and things for my Anniversary frock, and I nearly always used to get tar on it from the feet of the children who sat behind me (laughs) I remember, they used to put lard on my dress to get the tar off. Yes, I went to Sunday School. I can't remember who our teachers were, not till when I got upstairs, in the senior classes. Mrs Slatcher was there, and Peggy Collishaw I think, but I can't remember any of the other teachers. The Youth Club there was started for my age group by Mr and Mrs Slatcher. I went to the Youth Club till I was well in my twenties 'cos we still went to the Drama Group. We danced in the big room at the Sunday School and I can remember when from Chapel they used to have the Bazaar. They'd have stalls and the women worked all through the winter, cos I can remember the women coming down to Grandma's. They used to sit and sew things for the Bazaar. I assume that Grandma went to other houses as well. They did go round to different houses and sew, and make things, and they had Jumble Sales to make money for the Church. In the big room, the pews were at the side, and they used to fit the stalls on the wood that went over the top of the pews. They'd have all sorts of things that they sold, they made like lavender bags and things like that. Then they had concerts, and the men's weekend, and they'd sing various songs and act (laughs). During the War I must have gone to evening services with my Mother and we used to go across to the Sunday School and have an hour's hymn singing. My Mother was once a Sunday School Teacher there because she'd got a silver teapot that they gave her from Sunday School when she got married. I can remember there was a picture of Jesus talking with all these children round him and there was every race I would think depicted. Of course people did missionary work, and sometimes they had missionaries come to talk to us.

I always liked living in Hasland, well I suppose I didn't know anywhere else so it were fine (laughs).

ROY JACKSON

My memory in Hasland from a child is incredible. I can still remember my Grandma Potter wheeling me down Hasland Green in the rain in a pushchair, when we used to have these hoods with a piece that came halfway up, and I can remember facing the rain, and the rain coming over that.

I can also remember when I was small, having a spinning top, one of those that you pressed up and down. Course you'd got very simple things like a whip and top, you never see whips and tops now. I'd got Meccano and a Hornby train set as well.

You didn't get a lot of presents at Christmas, but you got a small one from every member of the family. I mean, you used to get an apple and an orange in a stocking, and a new coin, and one present from your parents. You used to have them all in a pillowcase. I went down one morning and there was a dog there for me, they'd bought me a pup, how they'd kept that a secret I don't know. They'd wait till I'd gone to bed you see.

Before we took the bakery we used to go up to my Grandma and Grandad Potter's house on Christmas Day and they lived up Hasland Green. Next door to them lived my Auntie Fanny and Uncle Sam, he was a masseur and he used to do all the miner's injuries. We used to go to Grandma and Grandad Potters for dinner and then in the afternoon we went straight down to Ashfield Road to my Grandma and Grandad Jacksons, and all the family used to make a lot of it.

Grandma and Grandad Jackson originally came from Leicestershire, Coalville, a place called Battram. They lived in Ashfield Road and they had their four kids there. My Dad was the eldest, then there was Uncle Walter, then my Auntie Dorothy who died, and then there was Cyril who took the bakery. In 1944 they moved onto Hampton Street, took the bakery and my Grandma and Grandad went with them. Then these Christmas parties carried on at Hampton Street at the bakery.

My Grandad worked at Grassmoor Pit and then he was watchman at Bryan Donkins. My Dad worked at Bryan Donkins and my wife Mavis' Dad worked there as well. I can remember when my Grandma and Grandad had their Golden Wedding they had their do at Sunday School. They were big missionary collectors all my young life. Course my Grandma lived till she was 90 and then she fell downstairs at the bakery there, she was reaching for a light in the dark. She died in January 1966 and my Grandad Potter up The Green, he died on my birthday.

You used to see the people going up to St. Paul's Church when my Grandma lived at Hasland Green, everybody who went up to church used to stand talking to you if you were stood at the gate there. You knew everybody. She lived there till my Grandad died and then she came to live with us at Farnsworth Street. I can remember watching funerals come past my Grandma's house. There was no cremation then, and it was the black horses and cart coming past, yes, they used to be all walking behind it. That's aging me isn't it? But they were lovely days, nobody had any money. I mean when I come to think what money we'd got at home. Now when people say to me 'You've got this and you've got that' I say 'Aye I've been on the other side of the fence as well'.

We had Easter Eggs but nothing like they have now, these decorated things today. Just plain, not even chocolate inside them. Then we ended up making them, 'cos we used to make them at the bakery. We'd decorate them with kid's names and put sugar rolls and lay fern on them. Oo it was a job though that. You see these moulds that we used, they didn't have plastic then, they were a shiny chrome, and if you'd got one blemish it'd crack your egg and that'd be it. But then the supermarkets started making them cheaper, and so forth, so it was a waste of time.

I remember going to Eyre Street School at four years old, when we went on our own, my Mother only took me for a day 'cos there was no traffic. There was Ian Batty, Bill Wild and myself, we used to go to school at four years old without our parents. The first class was Miss Ball in the nursery and then we went on to Miss Swan and Miss Cooper etc. Mavis and I started school on the same day. I can remember that we had bead boards and counting frames. We also had slates and chalk and when you'd done a lesson you rubbed it off. That was, till we got old enough for exercise books.

Mavis and I both went on to Hasland Junior School. Mr Keeton was Headmaster then, when we went, 'Buster' as we called him. Mr and Mrs Randle were the care-takers in that stone house next to it when we were there. The first teacher we had in there was Miss Cowley, then we went up to Miss Brown, then Mr Pearson, and then Miss Pickard. They all taught us. Miss Brown lived in Ashfield Road. Her father was Brown the builder and they had that big house at the bottom of Meakin Street, Ralph Jackson had that after them. Their workshop, workyard, was on that land just before you get to Ashfield Road, there's a big long drive there with garages on it, not 50 yards away, well that was Brown's woodyard. Browns built the houses in Burgess Close, you know.

When we moved from the Junior School, Mavis went up to Hasland Hall School and I went to Tapton. We left that school the year that War broke out and from the outside it's never changed.

We always lived on Farnsworth Street, and Randalls builders built that house. We had an outside toilet and the bath was hung up in the shed and we had to have a bath in the kitchen, you'd put a gas ring on to make the water warm. I was 21 years old before I lived anywhere where there was a bathroom and an indoor toilet, and that was when I was in the R.A.F. We'd these allotments at the back which they've now built on. We used to play on the allotments all the time and at that time they were all occupied and used. I always remember, Alan Hopkinson lived in the top house, and they'd a garage, and Stewart Brown had a big car in there. He was one of a very few people in Hasland that'd got a car at that time, and it stood in that garage right during the War. He never used it 'cos he couldn't get petrol. Yes, I always remember that, the smell of oil and that car, when you walked into that garage. To get into Hasland Park we used to have a short cut over the wall that is still at the top of Farnsworth Street, and we forced some railings apart to get into the Park. At the top there, on the corner, was Tommy Lowe's Farm, and Eastwood Park Drive was his farm paddock down to his fields. Tommy Lowe's sister Dorothy, taught me at Tapton.

Both Mavis and I went to the Methodist Church Sunday School morning and afternoon. Then you see when we went to the Youth Club Mrs Slatcher coaxed quite a few of us to go to Chapel on Sunday night. We used to go up to their house after Chapel for a cup of tea and a biscuit. They were lovely days they were. I can remember some of our Sunday School teachers. There was Peggy Collishaw, Violet Newman and Dora Wheatcroft's sister, Marjorie Wheatcroft. Course Winnie Apperley taught at Sunday School as well and played the piano. Eileen Greatorex played the piano as well, and she ran that pantomime for years. My Grandma and Grandad Jackson were superintendents of the main Sunday School then, when we first went to the Sunday School. Mrs Slatcher was superintendent eventually.

When we went on holiday we only went to Blackpool and places like that. I once went to Morecambe with my Mother and Dad and we met Mavis and her Mother and Dad but we didn't talk then. No, I didn't talk to girls then (laughs). We met at Heysham that day. I was a shy little boy then and have been ever since (laughs). We always went on the train and you carried your little metal bucket and spade, no plastic bucket, and that's all the child carried 'cos the father carried the cases. I'll always remember going to Blackpool, 'cos we used to see who could see the Tower first, 'cos you saw the Tower before you saw the sea. My Uncle Horace's brother or was it his uncle, kept a boarding house in Blackpool and that's where we always stayed. Then our Sunday School teacher, Marjorie Wheatcroft and her husband Len Carr, they took a boarding house and we went and stayed there. That was 1949, yes it was, we were twenty. Aye, wonderful days they were.

We used to cycle round on bikes a lot. Mavis and I cycled to Matlock once and when we started out it was a beautiful day, and we got to Matlock and the heavens opened and it thundered and lightened. We had to ride back through all this rain and we were saturated when we got back. I don't know how old we'd be then, in our early teens probably.

I've very happy memories really in Hasland. Mavis and I have said, we lived through the War but we still had wonderful times. The Youth Club at the Methodist Church started when we were fourteen and that was marvellous, it was a godsend, it really was. We used to pay, I think it was threepence a week. We met twice a week and of course we'd football teams, cricket teams, they did everything. The girls used to do embroidery and the boys did woodwork. Plastics were just coming in then and Norman Eyre ran a plastics class. You see, that'd be during the forties when plastic started coming in and replacing bakelite. I never went to that class but I went to the woodwork class. You see Mr and Mrs Slatcher, although they were very, very keen and we used to think they were strict, we were their kids 'cos they'd no children. They did a wonderful job, they didn't get paid for it. We'd 150 members at one stage and they got no pay. Then you see there was Peggy Collishaw and people like that running it, 'cos it ran on from Sunday School.

When we were at the Youth Club, there used to be a place called The Hut at Darley Dale, it was a wooden hut and we used to go there every year over a weekend. The lads dormitory was next door to the girls, well there were knot-holes you see, you used to peep through. I can remember that as clear as a bell, every girl that I saw through that hole (laughs). I always remember one night, there was a lad named Cliff Partridge. We went to bed and he shouted 'Who's had my bloody blankets' (laughs) and Mrs Slatcher said 'Who was that swearing?' 'Cos you didn't swear in those days, and there was a deathly silence. That'd be during the War that would.

It was a big blow to me when they knocked down the Sunday School on Chapel Lane. Hopkinson bought it, he did, yes. I remember him buying it. I was told that when he purchased it, he wasn't going to be allowed to build houses on it, but they're building on it now so they just waited you see. I mean they'd just had a kitchen built on that must have cost a lot of money and there were some wonderful function rooms. There was a stone on the building that was dated eighteen hundred and something and I remember the centenary in 1942. When you come to think, if there had been anybody with enough money to develop it, it would have been marvellous, the function rooms in there, that big concert room for a start. Then the Sunday Schoolroom next to it and all those rooms upstairs. I often wonder what happened to that organ upstairs in there, it was a nice organ that was. Cos Sunday morning I used to play at Chapel before the main service, then we'd come out. Then in the afternoon the seniors used to be upstairs at the Sunday School and I used to play that organ upstairs there. My biggest regret in life that, packing up lessons at fourteen. But it does seem a shame that that's gone, that building, it could have been a wonderful function place. The only problem would have been parking, it would now, yes. But that was a wonderful building set-up, alright, it wanted some money spending on it, but there was no subsidence in it as far as I know. No, it was marvellous.

I remember the old Baptist Chapel on Eyre Street as well, the Tin Tabernacle which used to be there, the 'Tin Tab' as they called it. I once went to the Temperance Society Meeting there, about four of us went. Joyce Allison's Dad took that and the next time I saw him he was in the Devonshire with a pint! It s true that, aye.

We took the bakery on Hampton Street in 1944, we retired in 1993 and I think our Trevor bought Mason's Bakery at Brampton in about 1995 and went up there. At one time we'd got the hardware shop as well. My uncle Cyril who had the business before me always walked with a limp, that was a motorbike accident. We'd got these, they were like plywood boxes with an opening lid which we used for deliveries and I used to wheel it round. I used to call at Slinns, who had the Post Office, then Darnells. Then I d go across the road to Woodheads and empty all these loaves under the window, they used to have 'em stacked under the window. We used to deliver down Kent Street and York Street, believe it or not. They couldn't walk up the street. I remember once, you know the dip down Kent Street, well I decided to sit on the barrow, and I lost it. (laughs) I lost control of it and we hit Moseley's wall, well I hit Moseley's wall, never mind the barrow. There was bread all over, and the wheels were all cocked up, and I finished up nearly in Moseley's garden. (laughs) I used to finish work at 4 o'clock on a Tuesday just after the War, and I had to then get the bus to get to Chesterfield, to the Railway Station, 'cos there were no cars, and catch the 5 o'clock train to Sheffield. I went to Sheffield Bakery School and I used to catch the 9 o'clock train coming back. Many a time I've come back in the guard's van because it was just going out of the station, and other than that there wasn't another for hours. Then Jack Aldread who used to be a baker at Grassmoor, he started a bakery school at Woodhead's old bakery at the back of the old Woolworths. We used to go there, and then he moved on to Hadfields at the top side of the market, it used to be Hadfields butchers and bakers there, and we used to go in their bakery. Then Jack packed up, and a bloke used to read to us, and I thought 'I can read that at home'. But there is not a bakery school in Chesterfield now, no.

The bakery is now in the Old Chapel on Newall Road up Brampton, and they'd still got the original tiles in there when our Trevor took it. Our shop on Hampton

Street was opened by Allens in 1902, and so was Hallam's hardware shop 'cos they were cousins. Mr Allen and Mr Hallam were cousins, and they both opened up in 1902, which is obviously over a hundred years ago. It was just about one hundred years old when it was knocked down, that bakery.

During the Second World War, apart from the obvious deaths and so forth, we had a wonderful time. Cos we were ten when it started. You were on rations but, I don't know, everybody seemed to healthy, there was no junk food or loads of sweet stuff. I mean when we took that bakery, Mr Allen who had it before us, never applied for a fat sugar ration. When we took it, my uncle Cyril had to rely on old bakers that he'd known for years to let us have these things and we used to go round buying off them. I mean we used to make scones with jam hoping we could get apricot jam so it didn't show as much. We used to make pink scones with that jam (laughs). We'd so little sugar that we were able to make our customers, as a treat, a swiss roll once a fortnight. But bread, we couldn't keep pace with bread, oh no we couldn't keep pace with bread. It was very brown you know, 'cos they used as much of the wheat as they could. Gradually as War ended it got whiter and whiter and then you got the difference from the sort of dirty colour. It was only 'cos it had got that bran in it. Mavis' Mother used to work on the ration books at the Town Hall. Of course we had air-raid shelters. In Farnsworth Street there were at least four families put all these Anderson shelters up, everybody had got one in their back garden, but they put four together in that allotment and made it into like a social club. We'd got no electricity in there, you only had candles and night lights. We used to love to get down there and play as kids, they didn't want us to go in, but I think we got a key from somewhere and we used to sneak in. You see we had to carry gas masks to school during the War. We did get bombed a bit, 'cos they tried to bomb the railway line at the bottom of Storforth Lane. They went either side of it, and there was one dropped, you know where that garage is on Marriott's Trading Estate well just below that. There was a crater there where one just missed that railway line. As you go down Langer Lane, on that corner where they called it the golf links, there used to be a great big crater where this bomb had dropped. But nobody got injured. Everybody used to come from far and wide to have a look at that crater. They were after the Railway Sheds that's what they were after, they bombed either side of the railway, but they didn't hit it. When there was that raid on Sheffield we could see it all, it was just as if it was in Chesterfield. It was like a huge firework display with all these search lights searching for the aircraft, and they used to shine like silver when the light hit the aircraft, so the guns could shoot at 'em. I watched that in Mrs Batty's backyard, one Sunday night. They did quite a lot of damage, to the steelworks and that, yes they did.

I can remember most of the shops in Hasland. Marcos was Miss McKays, that drapery shop, then there was Wilbourne's chemist next door, and then there was a shoe shop, Harolds. Below there used to be a dairy shop which is now the Café. Teagues had it at one time. Next door was Lenny Lee and his mother's sweet shop, and then Mrs Clark had it. Then there was Mrs Needham drapery shop which then became Marriotts, and next door was the paper shop. Then there was Woodheads which became Hagganbachs, and then became us, we bought the lease from Hagenbachs. Next there was Redfern's butchers on the corner. There were nine butchers in Hasland when we were kids, I could name em all and they all did well. Then on that corner next to the butchers was a hairdresser. Then there was Jack Carrs cobblers shop. Before it was Jack Carrs it was Miss Sedgewick's drapers shop that sold dresses, and they moved across the road to the top of York Street. Then Lowes bought that shop, Charlie Lowe and his wife and family took it up. Then there was the post office, and next there was Smiths men's hairdressers and then there was Darnell's greengrocers. Next there was Miss Parke's Shop, you know that little shop that Ralph Chambers had, that was Miss Parkes' little sweet shop. Then there was Gillings hairdressers and he had a women's department, next there was Miss Cope's little confectionary shop, Coppings, Shentalls and then Norman's butchers. Colin Adams was the only butcher without a shop, he used to have his making up place up the back of the Cinema. Yes , he used to be in there, but he never had a shop, he just had an old Jowett van.

On the top corner of Kent Street was Thompson's printers and on the corner of York Street and Hampton Street was a shop called the India and China shop. Then there was the butchers opposite the India and China that was Fearns before it was Philip Barnes. Halfway down York Street there was Waring's little provision shop, and then Gothard's butchers was at the bottom, which is now a chip shop. Then down at the bottom of Eyre street, on that corner, where the plant shop is now, that was Mr Jones he was a provision man, a grocery shop, he used to take his stuff out on a bike. There was another fish and chip shop halfway down York Street, that was Walls.

Opposite the Devonshire was the Co-op butchers and next to that was Sharp's fish and chip shop. There was also a greengrocers shop, Godfrey Normans, after the terraced houses. Course there was Geoff Brown's butchers on the top of Calow Lane. Then as you went down to Chapel Street, there was Norman's butchers shop. They had a bakery at the back, because when we first took our bakery we hadn't got a freezer and we used to buy frozen egg from them. We used to go to Mr Normans, take the tin opener to open this big tin of eggs, and scoop some out and put it in a bucket and take it back to the bakery (laughs) By the time you got back, if it was a warm day, it had melted nicely to use it. Prior to that, you see, during the War we used dried egg, we used to use this powder.

Yes, there were a lot of shops in Hasland.

At one time there were seven or eight farms in Hasland, the majority of those have gone now. When you went down Calow Lane, on your left was Hawkins farm, just round the bottom of Hoole Street, and then opposite Ashfield Road was Billy Stevens farm. Right at the bottom of Calow Lane, where the little bridge is was Hall's smallholding. Then up Hasland Green, of course there was Charlie Hollingworth's farm, and then Heathcotes had a farm both sides of the Green. There was Booths of course down Churchside, which I think is still classed as Hasland.

Then you'd got Lowes on Hasland Road at the top of Eastwood Park Drive, and then Fisher's farm, up that road opposite St Leonard's Drive, all their land used to run up the side of Hasland Road.

There used to be two old cottages at the end of Chapel Street near the Devonshire, and I think one was a blacksmiths. There used to be a cottage further round Chapel Street, near Sunday School, and the chimney sweep lived there. He was the only one for years, in Hasland, his name was John Glover. Then down below there was Vardy's cottage. I'm surprised they let them pull the Old Hall down, which was on Calow Lane, there was a lot of history attached to that. They used to say that there were passages from there to Hasland Hall. Then when you went round Handby Street corner there were some cottages there before they built that new one. There used to be some bungalows as well, you know where Hasland Cinema used to be, well in between the Cinema and the Shoulder of Mutton there were two cottages, you went down steps to them.

Opposite the beeroff down Calow Lane, there s two cottages set at an angle. Billy Vaines lived in one with his wife and Arthur Boyden lived in the next one. They were both horse and cart men with greengroceries. They both used to have different areas. There was Darnell's greengrocers on Hasland Green which was a big shop and there was Godfrey Norman next to Marsh's chip shop on Mansfield Road. They all did well. Cos all the village used to go to 'em, yes. Well you see Billy Vaines, his father lived up Saunders Row there, Storforth Lane Terrace, that's where he used to keep his horse and cart up there. Now Arthur Boyden, he kept his horse and cart at his cottage on Calow Lane, there were stables, I would imagine those stables are probably still there. He used to go and deliver up Ashfield Road when my Grandma and Grandad were there. My Grandma always used to take bread out for the horse. You know how horses used to stand outside, they didn't have to fasten 'em up, well if that horse saw my Grandma go down, and he was at the bottom of the street, well Arthur would have to rush up and fetch him back 'cos he'd gone up after the bread. My Grandma always had a slight heel on her shoe and they were tiled passages, so it used to hear her clomping down there with a bag, and of course he'd set off up the street. (laughs) Mr Hawkins at one of the farms down Calow Lane always brought our milk with a horse and cart. The milk was still warm from the cow, aye, and it were lovely milk. You got none of these diseases then because you were immune to em. When I left the bakery, just before we retired 11 years ago, I said to our Environmental Health Officer, I said 'You're killing everybody's immunity' and he says 'Roy, I know that, you know that, go and tell these people in Whitehall and Brussels. They keep piling it up on my desk, as soon as we implement one lot of rules there's another lot come in.'

It was marvellous growing up in Hasland, it was a village then, a lovely village and everybody knew everybody. I noticed this just before we finally left Hasland. Cos you see I had only left Hasland previously for two years when I went in the R.A.F., apart from that I had all my life working and everything there 'cos our business was there. People in Hasland used to marry people in Hasland. It used to take me two hours to walk up Hasland front 'cos of people I knew, now I can walk up Hasland front and wonder who they all are. I don't know anybody.

EVELYN HOLLINGWORTH

What's your earliest memory?

Well I've got a brother who is five years younger than I am and I remember we lived at the bottom of Storforth Lane near the Post Office. When Raymond was being born I was taken up to my Grandma's and she lived in an old cottage at the side of the Devonshire Arms in Hasland. It's a bungalow now, but it was an old cottage and she lived there, and I stayed with her and then a friend of my Mum's took me to Mansfield and that's what I can remember.

I can remember my Grandma Bingham buying me a black doll, it had such a beautiful face and it was all dressed in white. Someone else bought me a doll and it was in a box. They used to sell dolls then which were fastened in a long box. My Grandma used to do the shopping on a Saturday after tea. The markets and the shops in Chesterfield closed about nine o'clock at that time. They used to have a horse-drawn, I don't know what you'd call it, carriage, like a bus I suppose, to take them to Town. I can remember all the stalls having like a gas flare, it warmed round the stall and it also gave light you know. She did her week's shopping then, and it must have took her till the next morning to put it all away, I think. She used to take washing in. She used to wash for Railwaymen, they were bib and brace overalls, oh God, it must have been like ironing cardboard. Her kitchen was a big kitchen, and you had one table in the middle for eating and the other one was for ironing. Really hard work it was. When you think how you shove it in the washer now. You know they used to bake as well. I was telling my son Stephen the other night that when we were kids we always had a cooked supper. We had a cooking range so the oven was always hot. My Mum used to put allsorts in the oven and especially when my Dad was on afternoons, so that he had a hot meal to come home to, you know. We had potatoes and onions, and then she'd spread some cheese on with a bit of bacon. All sorts of things she'd put in the oven that wanted cooking for a long time.

We moved from Storforth Lane to Henry Street in Grassmoor because my Dad worked at the pit. I think I would be about seven then.

We went to the Methodist Chapel in Grassmoor till I was sixteen. I went to the Sunday School there as well.

At Christmas time, my Mum always made a fuss at Christmas. She'd start in October making mince meat, puddings and Christmas cake and yes we'd always a houseful for Christmas. In fact I wouldn't say there was an awful lot that was bought, but my Mum would make things. She'd either knit you a new cardigan or make you a dress, something like that, lots of things.

When I was a kid we always had a good time on Bonfire Night as well, and my Mum always made bonfire toffee, parkin and we had roast potatoes. But the best that I can remember, it was when Charlie and I were married before we had Stephen, we'd some friends at Cutthorpe. They had a smallholding, and we'd go down a long winding road right to the bottom, last place God made I think down there. They'd got twins who were born on Bonfire Night, so of course we always went and had a party. It was unbelievable. We'd go in and there'd be a kitchen-full of folks. It was an old range, you know the oven would be choc-a-bloc with potatoes, a great big frying pan with fried onions and sausages, a great big tub of margarine on the table. Our friend used to open the oven door and he'd say 'Catch' and he'd throw you a jacket potato (laughs) In the hearth all the skins were there, I would have gone absolutely bananas if it'd been me. Then we all used to go up to The Peacock for a drink, and we used to smell dreadful 'cos of the smoke but it was wonderful. It really was (laughs).

When I was about eleven, that was the first time we went on holiday for a week. My Mum had to work really hard and save because there were no holidays with pay. She had to save to take us on holiday and she also had to save to have money to cover my Dad's wages when we got home. We used to go to Blackpool and we'd go to the Tower, the circus. Yes it was fabulous really.

My Dad had some friends that lived in Hardwick Wood at Wingerworth and when he was on the day shift on a Sunday we'd walk from Grassmoor up there for a picnic.

My Father worked at Grassmoor Pit, he was a loco driver. In fact, when I would be about ten, if my Dad had to work extra hours my Mum would cook something and I'd go with a basket. I'd go down Chapman Lane, and I used to go to the signal box and this old man worked the signals. Mr Brooks his name was, and I used to go up there and I used to sit in there and wait for my Dad coming up on the train. Everything shone, the floor shone, the brasses on the big levers they shone, you know, and sometimes my dad would say 'Do you want a ride'. I'd go, and he'd lift me onto the Loco and we'd go as far as Grassmoor Station, that's where the scrap yard is now. On that road up there at Mile Hill there's a big house called Herne House, and when I was a little girl that was one of the bosses at the Pit, it was his house. They always had a garden party every year, and I can remember going there. I think his name was Mr Swallow if I remember rightly, and when they had a new loco, they called this loco Jean, that was after Mr Swallow's daughter. That would be in the early thirties.

Just down the road was Telmere Lodge which is now the Winsick Arms. Yes now, Mr Bradley my Dad's boss lived there. Oh it was a beautiful house, it was lovely, big staircases you know, it was beautiful wood. Now, when you go in it's all bitty bobby, I don't know. It was a beautiful place, really lovely.

As I talk to the friends that I've got now and how strict their parents were with them, I realise how modern my parents were. I mean, they loved to dance. They used to take me to dances and they'd have a baby sitter for my brother. I can remember one New Year's Eve and they had a dance in the Village Hall. There was a brass band for the old time dances and a modern dance band for the modern dances. I can remember going there but only once.

I started School at Hunloke with living at the bottom of Storforth Lane, but I wasn't there very long before we went to Grassmoor and I started at Grassmoor School. Then they changed the system and I had to go from Grassmoor to North Wingfield until I was eleven. Then when I was eleven we had to come back to Grassmoor to the Senior Girl's School. One thing that always stuck in my mind was the headmistress, and her name was Miss Cresswell, and it's not many years since she died. She was strict, but she was fair, you know. I left there when I was fourteen.

I went to Kay's Commercial College for nine months and that was right up the top of Saltergate in Chesterfield. Then I got a job at Wigfalls in Stephenson's Arcade in the office there. They used to sell push-bikes and prams and that sort of thing. Then when the war broke out they finished us all because they wanted all the staff that would be able to take over collecting, as the men collectors were called up into the Army. So I left there and I got a job at Swales on Sheffield Road. I stayed there, now then, perhaps two years, yes, two years. Then I got a job at Pearl Insurance at Clay Cross and I stayed there till I was married. I only left work then because the office closed, the office in Clay Cross closed. Then after two years Dianne was born, and she'd be five when I went back to work at the Pearl. I stayed at the Pearl until I was expecting Stephen. Then when he was seven I got a job at the Royal London 'cos I was sending them all crazy to go back to work. I stopped there till I retired. I used to help to take the milk round too, I did that sort of between jobs, I didn't like that at all, not at all, no. Everybody used to have their milk delivered in those days. I know when Charlie's Mum and Dad used to take the milk, your milk round was allocated to you. We used to take both sides of The Green, Smithfield Avenue and Hampton Street. We just had certain areas. Later Charlie bought his cousin Colin Heathcote's milk round when he went into a bigger farm. They had a farm at Tapton, Balmoak Lane.

We were very lucky really when the War came. When the boys were called up and they came home on leave, we always made a point of all meeting up and going out to a dance while they were on leave. I don't remember any of the people that I was friendly with getting killed, but I mean you'd see the names in the papers. I suppose really we did have a good time. There were no buses after nine o'clock you had to walk home. You'd dance all night and then have to walk home (laughs).

We lived in Grassmoor until I was eighteen and then we came down to the Club. My Mum and Dad were steward and stewardess of the Miner's Welfare Club which was next door to St. Paul's Church. I got married from there and Charlie and I had that little cottage on the corner at Green House Farm, you know where Betty Heathcote lived. We'd been married just a few months when we got that. Actually it was two houses, two cottages, and we lived in both pieces at different times. The cottage where we lived on the corner, Green House Farm, next door lived the headmaster from Pilsley School Mr Bell. Every so often we used to have a party and they were a really lovely couple. Well our toilet was across the yard and I went across and I could hear them singing their heads off in our house and I thought 'We'll be in trouble tomorrow'. Anyway I went round to apologise the next day. I said 'I am so sorry if we disturbed you last night' and Mr Bell said 'We opened the window and we laid in bed and we sang with you' and I said 'Well that's brilliant'. (laughs) We had two bad fires at the farm up there, but we were away for the second one. The first one we were here, and the corrugated roofing exploded and burning pieces were hitting our back door. It was frightening. Well when they sent for the fire brigade we were looking out of the cottage window and this fireman got off with a hosepipe. He rolled it out and connected it up to the water system and it was just like a colander. It was just like a fountain and I thought 'Well that's not going to put much of a fire out is it?' (laughs) Charlie was working all day and all night and they were taking trailer-loads of burning hay right down the field away from the cottage.

We came to the Green Farm when Charlie's Dad was ill and he couldn't run the farm.

I know that Great Grandad Hollingworth asked for tenders to build the houses on Hampton Street, Kimberley Terrace, those six. He had those built and then he bought so many more down Kent Street. Then on the front facing the Park there's some more with bay-windows, I don't know which they are, but he owned some of those. He also owned the India and China Shop at the top of York Street. Then when you go down York Street there are two semis which used to be Police Houses well he had those built as an investment, and he had some arrangement with the Police that they were let to the Police.

I can remember some of the shops in Hasland. There was a hairdressers at the bottom of the Green I don't know what shop it is now it's changed hands. It was near to Miss Copes. It was a hairdressers, they were called Gillings, and my Grandma used to go and have her hair done on a Saturday morning. She'd take me with her. They had these great big iron things that they put on a stove and crimped it all up. You thought you were t'bees knees. I'd be about six or seven then so it would be round about 1930. On the front of Hasland there was McKays. Mr McKay and his daughter lived on The Green but they had the shop which is now Marcos. Harolds had a shoe shop on the front, I can remember that. Then there was a big two-windowed shop that used to be somebody called Needham. They used to sell dresses and wool and all sorts of things. That which is the pet shop now was a butchers. I know my grandma used to cook big joints of pork and take it across to the shop, and they used to cut it up and sell it. There was Coppings on the other side, old Mr Copping and his sister Ivy. There was a Shentall's grocer s shop on that corner as well next to Coppings. Then what is Kate's Pantry now that was Woodheads. Then on the corner of Hampton Street and York Street was what they called the Indian and China. That was like a grocery shop but a different sort of grocery shop to Shentalls if I remember rightly. I can remember going in there with my Grandma but I can't remember who ran it. Then there was Hallam's hardware shop next to Jackson's bakery and shop. I can remember Cyril Jackson moving in there. He made my twenty-first birthday cake, and it was the first one he made from taking over the business. Then on the corner of Kent Street there was Thompsons the printers. There was Mrs Thompson, I can't remember a Mr Thompson, but there was Mrs Thompson and then this son. The son was the Prisoner of War, Japanese Prisoner of War. There was a shop halfway down York Street that was called Kings. They had this shop just in like a front room. Then further down York Street was the butchers which was Bentons. Pickards used to have the shop at the Hasland Road end of Eyre Street and opposite that was Unwins butchers.

There was a little twisted cottage opposite here, Hicklins had it. The door was cock-eyed and the windows weren't square. This little old lady, Mrs Hicklin used to live there with her son. Then when the old lady died they pulled that down and they built two semis.

Tony Randall's Dad lived right opposite here, he was a character. He used to come across when the fruit was ready and he'd bring a little basket and he'd say 'Evelyn, I've just come to bring you a few apples' and I'd say 'That's very kind of you Mr Randall, thank you very much, what do I owe you?' 'Well, just give me twenty pence for the seed.' You had to pay him for the apple seed (laughs). Well when he died Charlie said 'All the old characters in Hasland have gone' and I can remember Stephen said 'No they haven't Dad, not while you're alive'.

DENNIS KNIGHT

Can you tell me what your earliest memory is?

My earliest memory. Well, it's perhaps a strange one, in a way, but I think it must be the last days of the First World War. I lived on Hasland Road then, and I can remember running into the house, 'cos I was only about four, and it was an air-ship flying over part of Chesterfield where we lived, and I was terrified, and I ran into the house. I think that was probably somewhere in 1918, which I think I could claim to be my earliest memory. I may have some more memories but I don't know what dates to put to them. I seem to remember people talking about it at some time or other afterwards, which dated it vaguely in my mind.

I was born at Hasland Road, and lived there 31 years till we came to Clarkson Avenue. We came here in 1946, the year after the end of the War, the year following the War.

I seem to have a memory which relates, as far as I was told, to the end of the First World War. Where we lived in Hasland Road you could look over what was farmland, Hardy's Farm, we used to call it, which is now a big housing estate, towards Wingerworth, and everywhere you could see were bonfires. Well. I've put two and two together since, and I think they were the peace celebrations after the First World War which were held in the year after, in 1919. So that's probably another one of my earliest memories. Whether I knew at the time what they were is a different story. I can see the bonfires now. The War was already on when I was born, and it would only have been over a month before I was four years old. The only thing I can remember is this air-ship thing, and I don't know then exactly what date it was.

I remember two things I think which probably blighted my life forever (laughs). I had a model bus, a London bus probably it would be, which I seem to think now was a rather detailed good model, which was a favourite until my Mother put her foot on it and squashed it flat (laughs). She was probably more upset than me (laughs). I had some soft toys, I remember a teddy bear and a dog which they tell me, I can only vaguely remember this, but I gave both of them a haircut with a pair of scissors one day and cut the hair short. Well I had these toys at the age of five cos I can remember the Summer after I was five, I was stricken with diphtheria and went into Penmore Hospital. When I came out, these toys had been taken away and destroyed, which broke my heart at the time. That's what they did in those days to combat infections and whatnot. Anything that could be destroyed, was, and I've never been the same since (laughs).

We played games in the street mainly. Our house, although the address was Hasland Road, the backs came out into Central Street. In those days there wasn't as much traffic on the main Mansfield Road as there is now. Central Street was really a quiet off-shoot because it wasn't a through road. We didn't go to the park because I suppose it was a bit too far away for a small child. Though I was attending schools in Hasland at Eyre Street and on The Green.

I started school in 1920. It'd be after the Christmas holidays, so it'd be January 1920, 'cos I'd have been five in the December before. I started on The Green which was, as far as I can see now, in two parts, an infant's section, and a senior section. After a shortish period, I don't know how long now, from starting school, we were moved down to Eyre Street. I was there nearly a couple of years when we were moved back to the Green again into the senior school, which was on the right-hand side of the gate, whereas I'd started on the left-hand side of the gate. There were two separate buildings with a common playground in between. But I don't know the official set-up, I think there must have been two separate schools. For instance, where I started, at the infant s, I don't think Daddy Boden had any control over that part. But later on, after we came back up from Eyre Street, it was all one school Daddy Boden was in charge of the lot.

I can remember my first teacher at Hasland Green was Miss Lowe who was the sister of the local farmer and milkman. Lowes supplied us with milk in those days, I don't know why I should, but I thought it was something rather wonderful to have our milkman's sister as a teacher (laughs). There was a Miss Allibone, I think she came from York Street, I remember her as one of the nice teachers. There was Miss Wheatcroft who lived opposite Lowe's farm, there were three sisters Wheatcroft and Ethel was a teacher at Hasland. She was a nice teacher, who encouraged one to do things. In fact I was in her class when I got the scholarship to the Grammar School. Down at Eyre Street I remember a Miss Cooper, an elderly teacher then who lived in York Street and had taught my Father years before, so you can tell how old she was. Adelaide Cooper. Miss Walton was the headmistress, I don't know where she came from, I didn't have much to do with her. She was reasonable to me as far as I remember. There was a Miss Ball, Ciss Ball they called her, who was a bit of a tyrannical-looking person, stern-faced and stern in nature, I was terrified most of the time with her. Very strict disciplinarian, that type. You hardly dare speak out of turn. Yet I suppose the time I was with her, it could only be a few months at the most 'cos I was only at Eyre Street a couple of years.

I seemed to be divided really with living a good half mile from the village, yes, it was a good half mile. I reckon it was three quarters of a mile from where we lived to the Green School. Spital was nearer than Hasland and although most of my relatives lived in Hasland, sometimes it seemed I knew more people in Spital than I did in actual Hasland. Then later on when I was going to the Grammar School my direction was away from Hasland all the time. Through Chesterfield, down Sheffield Road, so it gave a different outlook. Not that I had many new friends apart from those I knew at the Green School.

I went to the Grammar School in 1925, I can remember that. It was a mixture of good and bad really, some of the masters were kind and gentle and others were terrible ogres (laughs) which I've not much time for, to this day. Some of the sarcastic ones seem to have blighted my life and given me a hatred of school-teachers in general, which is perhaps not quite fair. I can remember one good teacher in particular. He was a science master for physics and chemistry in the sixth form, which I'm sure ignited the spark in me of wanting chemistry as a career which subsequently came through. I was lucky to get a job in that field but I'm sure it was the master that inspired it in the first place. Whereas another teacher with a different character might not have done so, could have been boring or tyrannical or whatever. After I'd started work at Sheepbridge in 1933, I was apprenticed, they did an apprenticeship scheme and part of the set-up was you attended night school to take a course in metallurgy. You could either do it at the Technical College, which would take five years, or you could take it at the University of Sheffield where you could do it in four years. Well, to my mind, four years seemed better than five years, so although it was a bit of a chore travelling to Sheffield four nights a week that's what I opted to do. Well in the end it turned out successful because I got a minor degree after four years, and I got what they call an Associateship in Metallurgy. This was the same exam that the full-time students, full-time bachelor students took. But of course we didn't put the hours in, ours was called a part-time degree. It doesn't exist now, they don't do it at Sheffield, you can get a similar one from the Institute of Metallurgists, A.I.M. they call it, Associate of the Institute of Metallurgists.

Our house on Hasland Road was a simple three up, three down, whatever they call it (laughs) no bathroom. Friday night was bath night in a tin bath in front of the fire (laughs). The funny thing is, my Dad, who worked at Grassmoor Pit, before the days of pit-head baths, he used to have to bath in the same fashion yet I can never remember seeing him in the bath. But I mean, even if you had a cleanish sort of job down the pit all day, you'd get dirty, dirtier than the average person. The pit-head baths came to Grassmoor fairly early I think, they were one of the first in the country to have them, and, well all the chaps, my Dad and all his mates they thought they were wonderful. Funnily enough, uncle David Knight, was one of the first three properly appointed bath attendants. He'd worked in the pit before but when these baths were opened, he was probably getting near retirement, I don't know, I don't know much detail about that. He was older then my Dad. With my Dad being a member of such a large family, I've heard him say there were twenty years difference in age between him and his eldest brother. My Dad was one of the younger ones.

We really celebrated Christmas. I seem to remember Christmas Day as a very happy time. We only got one present, not like today, but I never felt deprived (laughs). I got a stocking with an apple, an orange and some nuts in, which you could get at any time, not just Christmas, but it seemed special then. My Dad always had a cigar and I always associate cigar smoke with Christmas. We stayed at home. I don't think there was much going to tea amongst the family because it would be too expensive as there were so many of them (laughs). It'd take you all year to go round them. We had Easter Eggs, I don't remember any special celebrations apart from church services, I always liked the Easter hymns. I went to Sunday School at Spital, it was attached to the Church of England. The Crooked Spire was the mother church. Spital was what they called a mission church. It doubled as an ordinary day school in the week, but on Sundays they could erect screens and what-not and turn it into a place of worship. Later on when I was a bit older I used to go to the services at the Parish Church, The Crooked Spire. I went until I was about eighteen and I'd started work by then. Sometimes I had go to work on a Sunday morning which seemed to put paid to church-going. I was probably half a heathen anyway by then (laughs). Another thing I remember about that. I'd had a bicycle for some time and I can remember when I first asked my Father if I could have a bike. I don't quite know how old I was then, perhaps twelve or thirteen. He said yes I could have a bike, but there was no riding it on Sundays. This didn't bother me at the time anyway as I wasn't into going out on Sundays I suppose. But as I mentioned before when I started work and had to go in sometimes on a Sunday morning, the bike was the only means of getting there 'cos there were no buses. That put paid to the 'no biking on Sundays' rule. You see my life opened up at eighteen in those days (laughs). Yes, when I joined the Rambling Club, many years after, my Father never said anything, but I often wondered if he thought I'd gone downhill altogether (laughs). He was pretty broad-minded though, I don't think he bothered. I always wore a best suit on a Sunday not the scruffy old clothes that I tend to now.

I can remember one or two of the shops in Hasland. Coppings was always there (laughs). There was a little sweet shop just up The Green, between Coppings and York Street. There was Miss Copes but there was another little one a bit further on, before Copes came, but I can't remember who kept it. There were two Copes sisters, they were very attractive-looking these two sisters, course much older than me. I can't remember their first names. This other sweet shop, just a bit up on The Green from Miss Copes, was only a tiny shop, very small window, it was popular and used a lot. There was a barber's shop where I used to get my hair cut on my way home from school. Smith's it was. Haircuts cost me fourpence in the old money. When I started the Grammar School and called at a shop in town, the price was sixpence then, which I thought was terrible (laughs). That was Bolts somewhere near where The Winding Wheel is now. The Post Office was next to Mr Smith's and that was always Slinns I think. Oh, there was a shop in Hampton Street where they sold paraffin, Hallams that was. That used to intrigue me, I think it was the smell of the paraffin, pleasant one, well to my nostrils anyway (laughs) some people may not like paraffin (laughs). On the front at Hasland there was one called Laits which I think was a newsagents, it was a general sort of shop, they probably sold sweets as well. There were two sons, Frank and Gilbert. Frank Lait was in my class, Gilbert was a bit older, two or three years older so that I didn't know him so very well. I knew Frank Lait, he became a painter and decorator.

We went on holiday when I was young, but there was a period when my Father's financial situation wasn't so good and we couldn't afford to go away every year. There was a long period when we went every alternate year. We went to all the usual places that Chesterfield people did in those days like Blackpool, Morecambe, Cleethorpes, Skeggy, Scarborough. Scarborough became a favourite with me, partly because I think it's a nice place, and partly because it had got some sentimental value indirectly, because it's where my parents had honeymooned in 1910, nearly a hundred years since. They were married at the Crooked Spire. My Mother was a teacher there, a Sunday School Teacher, but my Dad of course was a Methodist same as the rest of the family. But after the second World War, later on in my life, I became motorised and of course we used to go further afield. That's when I discovered touring and I used to like Devon and Cornwall although I've been to other places as well. Wye Valley, Norfolk, Suffolk, the Yorkshire Dales. There's still some areas that I've not been to, which I shan't get to now.

I always remember I think my childhood was a happy one. I'd got lots of pals who I knocked about with. They changed over the years like most people's do. I played all the usual childish games of 'Cowboys and Indians'. Luckily there was a lot of waste ground just below where we lived, between us and what was the Co-op, Warner Street Branch. There were houses all down the main road to there, but at the back of the houses was not built on, and it was ideal for us to play on. There were fields and you could do all sorts of things there, but of course it's all built on now. I remember St. Leonards Drive, the road to Spital, was only like a dirt track in my earliest memories. I can remember them making a proper road of it and giving it a fancy name, St. Leonards Drive. I can remember the blacksmith's shop at the end of Chapel Lane, Redgraves it was. Eddie Redgrave, one of the sons was in my class. There again, I thought it was rather a unique feature somehow to have a blacksmith's son in my class (laughs). I don't know why, I'm sure. In those days, kids, I don't know whether they do these days, well they have tyres now, trundle tyres along the road but we had either wooden or iron hoops, bowls, we used to call them. If you had a metal one it was just like a rod bent into a circle and welded at one end. Well they very often broke at that point but you could take 'em to the blacksmith and for a matter of 1d or 2d he'd stick it together again. I've had many a one done like that. Redgraves later moved into the Town he had a blacksmith's shop just off Beetwell Street. Up one of those yards at the back of South Street. I don't know why they left Hasland. It would be to make way for where the Alms Houses are, that's where the blacksmith's shop was.

I was only about twelve when my Grandma Knight died. Although funnily enough I can picture her now, like an old-fashioned matriarch always dressed in black as I remember, which probably all the old ladies did in those days.

I was twenty four or twenty five when the Second World War started. Nowt but a lad (laughs). I can remember the Sunday morning that the Prime Minister, Neville Chamberlain announced the outbreak of war. There was just me and my Mother in the room, we both sat silently and when he'd finished speaking, my Mother just burst into tears. No word was spoken between us, but if you think about it, she'd already experienced the First World War. She'd gone through it all, rationing and looking after me as a squawling baby and that sort of thing. She'd be thinking would I be called up for this one, and all sorts of things would be on her mind. Of course Chesterfield was lucky in that they only got a few stray bombs, so we weren't troubled that way. We were troubled with aircraft going overhead to other places because the sirens would sound every time they were heading this way. That got us up, although we got a bit blase about that. I was then a member of the First Aid section based at Derby Road School, First Aid Party. Later they changed their name to rescue or something or other. There were a few incendiary bombs dropped at Newbold near Dunston Lane but they didn't do much damage. I think the local people managed to put them out. There were some bombs or a bomb dropped at the back of Storforth Lane, in the fields, Taylor's Fields we used to call it. Funnily enough this particular evening, a friend of mine, a school friend of mine, was at our house. He was working in Windsor then, but he'd come home. He lived in Walton Road with his parents and he was at our house when this bomb dropped. Well, it was comparatively near, it was only separated from us by the Storforth Lane Terrace pathway and from what I remember, he dived under the table instinctively whereas we ignaramuses just sat there doing nothing (laughs). But living in Windsor he'd heard a lot of bombs, he'd not suffered any damage or anything but they'd been close to. Then I was on duty at Derby Road on the night of the Sheffield Blitz in 1940 which happened to be my birthday. We were on duty but there was nothing doing in Chesterfield, so we were sort of fully dressed and equipped lying on a stretcher just getting some rest. They dropped some bombs in Hawthorne Street off Derby Road and we could hear them. We'd heard them bombing but there wasn't a deal of damage done then. They were just sleepless nights more than anything else.

My Mother worked, before she was married, worked in a confectioner's shop in Hasland. I'm not quite sure where, whether it was on the front, as they call it these days, or if it was just round the corner on The Green. But it was owned by a chap named Harry Elliott who had a shop also in Lordsmill Street opposite the Feathers Hotel. I can remember it very well cos when I went to Town with my Mother we always called there. Harry Elliott, who owned the shop, was a friend of my Grandfather's, how they came to be friends I don't know 'cos there was a bit of an age gap. But as I say, he owned the shop in Hasland and my Mother went to work there. It was before she was married 'cos I think that was probably how she met my Father. Father lived in York Street, with all the other gang of Knights you see. But in those days my Father, who was only in his late teens probably, had a coal business, he had a horse and cart and took coal around. This was before he went into the pit. As young men used to do then, he was dallying with the girls. He'd driven up to the shop with his coal cart, went into the shop to talk to my Mother, must have over-stayed his time, because he said somebody came rushing into the shop saying 'Walter, your horse and carts halfway down Hasland Road'. It had got fed up with waiting and gone off on it's own (laughs). Whether that's true or not, I don't know, Father said it was. I can quite believe it because it fits in with his courting days. My Mother used to like going to Father's house because there was always a houseful of 'Knights', even though a lot of them had left home, there were still a lot of them left.

In those days there were no buses. My Mother lived in the Town, it was just off the Market Place. In two places, the first one was Soresby Street near the Post Office, and then at the bottom of the Market, near to a pawnbroker's shop called Fieldsend's. I forget whose there now, well it's all in The Pavements. There were a series of yards, Wilcockson s Yard, it was called. My Mother said that they used to have to fetch the water from the pump in the middle of the Market Place. I can remember visiting my Grandparents down there. There were no buses from Hasland to Chesterfield then, so when my Mother had finished work the only alternative was to walk, unless she could get a lift in a wagonette or some privately owned vehicle. So my Dad had probably taken her home in the coal cart sometimes, I don't know (laughs). But apparently there was a wagonette, like the fore-runner of a bus service, which used to wait in Hasland until it was full and then they'd set off. You might have waited hours until it was full (laughs) if there weren't many customers. Cos remember there were hardly any houses then, it was just a country lane, in fact it was called Chesterfield Lane, it wasn't Hasland Road. Where we lived, the house was brand new when my parents went into it. My parents had got one modern feature, it was a porcelain sink in the back kitchen 'cos previous to that all sinks had been stone, stone slabs. It was gas lit of course, still that was modern in itself 'cos previous to that they'd had paraffin lamps.

My Dad didn't get a car till he was nearly sixty, he'd come out of the pits by then. He had to come out through illness, he was crippled with rheumatism and he lost a lot of weight. I think he never thought he' d work again. He was out of work all one Summer. He did make a recovery, so much so, that he even thought about trying to get another job. This was during the last War, about the middle of the last War. It was just about that time that open-cast coal was opening up in the Derbyshire area. There were adverts in the paper for experienced ex-miners or anybody who worked in the pits, to act as inspectors for the new opencast coal. My father thought it would suit him so he applied and he got it. He worked for what became the Coal Board for about the next twelve or thirteen years, until he retired just before his seventieth birthday. He never looked back, I never saw him so healthy all my life. Sunshine pits, he used to call 'em (laughs). That's the way we came to get a car because a job came up which would have been a very good promotion, but it required somebody able to drive. Well, my Father couldn't drive then, and they were strict about it. He would have suited the job in every way but he lacked driving experience. So he missed that opportunity but it spurred him to take driving lessons and he did. Much to his own amazement he passed his driving test and then he thought about buying a car. He hadn't got a car of his own then, he'd learnt to drive in the instructor's car. Well, as I say, he was turned sixty when he learnt to drive. I was thirty four and I thought 'Well if he can learn to drive so can I' (laughs), so that's how I came to learn to drive. That's fairly late in life these days to a young person, I suppose, but it had never bothered me, I didn't need one. Admittedly, it's one of those things, that once you've got it, it broadens your horizons, but if you haven't got it and you're not bothered about broadening you horizons, it doesn't matter does it?

My father was 71 when he died, which is not very old these days. He died in 1957. Then my Mother lived to be 91 nearly twenty years after. She died three years before I retired.

I think my childhood in Hasland was a happy one, it was a good place to grow up in. I enjoyed my time there.

MARGARET LEIGH-MORGAN

My Grandparents were Henry and Ann Hopkinson and my earliest memories of Hasland were of visiting Grandma Hopkinson on Sunday mornings with my father and playing a favourite board game called 'tiddlywinks' under the table with my sisters. The table was covered by a long chenille tablecloth so we were hidden from view. I can see Grandma's black shoes and long black skirt walking back and forth. I was rather in awe of her because of the way she dressed and her hair was drawn into a tight bun with a centre parting but she was very kind to us. Grandad would be standing at the gate smoking his pipe, talking to Dad. We had to be on our best behaviour. Their home was at Calow Lane in Hasland. My sister remembers that there was a smell of freshly baked bread as she walked through the village because everybody made their own.

Most of the children we knew had very few toys so we really didn't expect to own many. We were not a well-off family and toys were often home-made. Knitted or rag dolls for girls and wooden toys for boys. We had to share with siblings the toys we had, except for a special doll or rag book. Christmas was a treat and we looked forward to some toys then. A whistle or mouth-organ to blow or a tin 'clacker' in the shape of a frog which made a certain sound when it was pressed. Snakes and Ladders and Tiddlywinks were favourite board games. There was usually a pack of cards, suitably chosen according to age. Our brothers would have playing cards and a crib board and the younger members would have nursery card games or snap cards. Scrap books, Bibles, Prayer books and religious picture books were often given and I loved taking a new book to Sunday School. I longed for a blackboard and some coloured chalks and finally got one at Christmas when I was about eight. My sister found it behind my parents wardrobe and told me about it but that didn't spoil it, I just couldn't wait. I loved playing school and every flower on the bedroom wallpaper was a pupil of mine. I had a ruler, just like our teacher at school and gave some of them a hard time!

There were seasons for certain games, like whip and top in the summer and skipping ropes. Battledore and shuttlecock were for girls – a wooden homemade bat usually. Boys made bows and arrows or kites and if they were lucky, they could make a go-cart out of some old pram wheels and a wooden box. In the winter, we would knit or draw in the evenings or make a long rope with rainbow wool and a cotton bobbin. I think we called it French knitting. We were taught to sew at an early age and we would make kettle holders, handkerchief cases, needle holders, aprons, teacosy covers as Christmas gifts for our lucky relatives!

Our homes in those days were cold and comfortless compared with today, but we were used to them that way and didn't expect luxuries. It was the same for all our neighbours. The ceilings were usually high and therefore colder, but the living room was always heated by a coal fire which was the focal point. It was part of a coal range, and had an oven at the side and a back boiler for heating water. This was drawn off from a shiny brass tap. Quite a dangerous procedure. There was usually a brass fender round the hearth and a large fireguard, I can remember gathering round the fire in the evening and the coal would crackle and spark sometimes, lighting up our faces and feeling very cosy. It was quite a different feeling when the time came to leave it and go to bed in the rest of the house. Being a mining area, I cannot remember ever being short of coal, but some families were. The windows were large and draughty and the frames shook and rattled on a windy night, so they were covered with heavy curtains, which the coal dust would cling to. The floors were usually covered with lino and a rug would be made by hand for the hearth. That was one of our winter jobs, pegging a rag rug. Old coats and curtains would be cut into strips and pegged with a tool made from a wooden clothes peg. The base was a large piece of hessian and it was so hard getting the rags through that after an evening, the fingers would be blistered, but there was a certain satisfaction in finishing a row and they were bright and cheerful. In our home. There wasn't much room for furniture because there were nine children, but what we had was solid and hard wearing. The table was usually plain wood, covered with a heavy cloth when it wasn't being used, which wasn't very often.

The bedrooms were like very cold dormitories and we didn't spend much time up there in the winter. There were fireplaces in the bedrooms but they were only lit when somebody was ill. We had a candle in a metal holder with a looped handle to light us upstairs and the draught would cause the light to flicker and send weird shadows. It would send shivers up the spine of a small girl. Dangerous, too, but that was all we had so small girls had to grow up quickly and learn to be cautious. The main lighting was by oil lamps in those days. These had to be filled, the wicks trimmed and the smoke cleaned off the tall glass cover before it got dark and when the oil sometimes ran out, it was very spooky.

Later on, we had gas lights in the main room, on a bracket coming from a pipe in the wall. There was a small tap with which to turn on the gas. The gas was controlled by a mantel on the end, being a mesh cover which gave off a light when heated. Care had to be taken not to touch this mantel or it would disintegrate into powder. As with oil lamps, there was a glass cover to protect it and they could be plain or ornate, but again they needed cleaning every day.

We didn't have bathrooms and the lavatory was outside so it wasn't a good idea to need it in the night. For this reason, there was a chamberpot underneath each bed which needed emptying every morning. Chamberpots could be ornate, too. The one in the girl's room used to have pink flowers on but the boys had plain white. One of us had the job of tearing old newspaper into squares and hanging in the outside lavatory on a piece of string, as, if toilet tissue had been invented, it was considered a luxury at that time for us.

The kitchen, or scullery, had a deep butler sink and one cold water tap. The floor was usually stone slabs with just a doormat to stand on to protect the feet from cold. Washing and shaving was done at the kitchen sink. My mother had a wash basin and jug on a washstand in her bedroom. Bath night was Friday night and this was done in the zinc bath before the fire. I remember having our hair washed with Durbac soap and combed with a fine tooth comb, to keep the nits away. It was a hard, green block of soap with a disinfectant smell and suds that stung the eyes.

Friday night was also the night Mother dished out senna pods. She would put them in the teapot and the tea always tasted strange at teatime on Friday. As there was no school next day, we were cleansed inside and out.

Our underclothes consisted of a vest and a liberty bodice. This was like a round-necked waistcoat with rubber buttons right up to the neck. The buttons had to be rubber so that they would go through the mangle which was used to squeeze the water out after washing. We even slept in these two garments under our nighties as the bedrooms were so cold. In the morning, we would add bloomers with elastic in the legs and a flannel petticoat. Clean clothes were supplied on Sunday for church and they had to last the week.

Sunday morning early was special for us sisters. One of us was sent by Grace, the eldest and therefore in charge, to our parents bedroom to collect the sweets they had bought for us at the market the night before and Grace dished them out. (Not always evenly but I forgave her for that long ago!) We also collected a small leather case containing photographs and other treasures. These were to be treated very carefully and to keep us all quiet whilst mother and father had an extra rest. There were postcards with lace edging from various corners of the world. Brief First World War messages from soldiers of the family and a picture of our uncle, Private Rowland Heath 14387 7th Bn., Leicestershire Regiment, in army uniform. He died in battle on 14 July 1916 and is remembered with honour on the Thiepval Memorial. This made us feel very solemn and we would stare at it and remember him in silence. Then there was a small bonnet with lace trim and ribbon ties, wrapped in white tissue paper, which made us even more solemn. It had been a Christening bonnet for my parents second baby, Beatrice Madge Hopkinson who died of pneumonia at six weeks old. We knew how sad it made our mother and only Grace was allowed to hold it because it was so frail. The case also contained badges and buttons and medals and brooches. I wish I had it today but we don't know what became of it.

Our parents were born in the reign of Queen Victoria and in those days, discipline was very strict and there was a code of conduct which had to be followed. With nine children to bring up, there wasn't time for discussions and we had to do as we were told. One child had to help with the care of the next and we all had jobs to do. At the same time, we knew we were loved and cherished and felt secure.

My father was the kindest man I have ever known. Because my mother was always caring for a new baby, he would get up in the morning, light the fire, make the tea and take her up a very thin slice of bread and butter and a cup of tea. He would then get all the young children up and give them breakfast of fried streaky bacon and bread dipped in the fat and a cup of sweet tea. This would stick to our ribs and keep us healthy and warm. He would then sit us in a row, put on our high buttoned boots and come round with the button hook to button up our shoes, send us off to school and go to work in his shop. He had probably been to deliver newspapers long before it was light.

My father was also the medicine man. To visit a doctor cost 2/6d and a home visit cost 5/-d which working people could not afford so we visited the chemist instead. My father had a prescription for cough medicine and a cure for every other illness. For colds, he boiled up spanish onions and liquorice root and we would drink the mixture. Ugh! For coughs in the night, he would get up and mix butter, sugar and vinegar in a saucer, holding it over the warm ashes in the fireplace to soften it and we would eat it with a teaspoon. I did it for my grandchildren and it still works. Sometimes I had earache in the night and father would take a warm brick that was kept in the oven, wrap it in a piece of flannel and put it on my pillow. My mother would take me into her bed and in the morning, when the thin bread and butter and tea came up, I was given a taste and some of the tea would be poured in the saucer to cool and it was so special. Whooping cough was more serious and a piece of rope, soaked in tar, was tied loosely round the neck to ease the symptoms. Sore throat was treated by camphorated oil or goosegrease rubbed into the neck. Chest infections were treated with the same and a piece of thermogene tucked inside the vest. It used to itch so much, the cough was forgotten! Styes on the eye were treated with a dose of brimstone and treacle. The taste wasn't bad but it was very gritty. Elderflowers steeped in boiling water were the cure for headaches. It was said that chilblains could be cured by dipping the feet in the chamberpot, but we preferred running our bare feet in the snow. There always seemed to be plenty of that about in those days.

In the winter, we were all given a daily spoonful of Scott's emulsion or cod liver oil and malt to keep us immune and we all survived.

Monday was wash-day and this took place in the wash-house outside the back door. There was a sink, with cold water tap and a copper. This was a deep copper cauldron, enclosed in a brick surround, underneath which was a grate to make a fire to boil the water. The water could be pumped from an outside pump or obtained from the tap. A long process, taking a lot of energy and time. When the water was near boiling, soap or powder would be put in and stirred with a long copper stick and all the white clothes placed inside to boil and the wooden lid closed. After boiling, they would be fished out with the copper stick and ladle, and carried over to be rinsed in the sink. The remaining water in the copper was used for the coloureds and a brass ponch or wooden dolly could be used to work the clothes clean. Then the remaining water had to be ladled out and the copper dried. The final rinsing water would have a Reckitts blue dolly bag squeezed into it. The Reckitts advert always carried the slogan 'Out of the blue comes the whitest wash'. The clothes would then have to be put through the mangle and onto the line. Some collars and tablecloths needed starching at this stage and the starch had to be mixed first. Robin Starch was a powder which had to be made up like custard. A few spoonsful were put in a bowl and mixed with cold water, then boiling water poured on to make it thick and when diluted with cold water was ready for use. On wet days, the washing had to be dried indoors and would be hung round or over the fire and was a depressing sight.

After that it all had to be ironed with a flat iron that had been heated on the fire.

No wonder women dreaded wash-days and only had time to produce a makeshift meal.

My father was a Newsagent in Mansfield Road in Hasland. During World War 1 he also had to work down the coal mine. That was because he only had the sight of one eye and was not fit to join the forces. My mother had to look after the Newsagents and family at this time.

I went to Derby Road School and the teacher I remember most vividly was when I was about five and she was showing me how to knit. I dropped a stitch for the third time and she swung her hand and smacked me hard across my face. I was trying so hard and it was a shock that hurts even to this day.

My sister has a happier memory of a teacher at Derby Road school called Miss Ray who was always very kind to her.

My four brothers and eldest sister were born in Hasland between 1910 and 1917. They were baptised at St. Paul's Church by the Rev. W. V. Davies. They attended Hipper Street Infants School.

We all went regularly to Sunday School and often to church with our parents in the evening as well. I can remember quite a long walk across fields to church, but that may have been after we left Hasland. My parents liked to attend the Methodist Church, although they were married and we were all christened at St. Paul's Church. After the Sunday evening service, on summer evenings, people would make their way to Queen's Park in Chesterfield where they would parade in their 'Sunday best'. Men would wear straw hats like boaters that were called strawyards and we had a competition to see who could count the most. This was a good time for scrounging cigarette cards (from boxes thrown away or politely asked for from a smoker.) There were about fifty cards in a set and the boys liked footballers and cricketers. They would play a game of skimming in the playground and if one card landed on top of someone else's, they could claim it. The girls went for birds and butterflies and it was quite a thrill when a swapping session completed a set.

There was usually a Sunday School outing in the summer, which we all looked forward to and a picnic tea provided. This consisted of a paper bag (no plastic in those days) containing a thick sandwich and a thin piece of cake. There was probably a tea urn which provided our drink. Nothing fancy or fizzy.

Our family couldn't afford holidays when I was small but I remember day outings to Scarborough and Dovedale very occasionally. After we left Hasland, we used to return on train excursions to see my grandparents who lived in Lucas Memorial Homes, Mansfield Road, Hasland. I also had holidays with various Aunts and Uncles in Hasland.

We celebrated Christmas in a religious way as well as in a family group. It wasn't a long drawn out commercial event as it is now. Most people worked on Christmas Eve for at least part of the day and had to do the shopping in the evening after they had been paid. There were no fridges or freezers so the food shopping was left until the last day as well. My parents would do all theirs in the evening and then come home to prepare. We would be allowed to join in the preparations until bedtime and decorate the tree with sugar mice and real candles clipped on in tiny holders. So dangerous! We made paper chains and Angels and crepe paper balls. My mother would crawl up to bed about three in the morning, tired but happy. Santa always came downstairs at our house and (after drinking his jug of cocoa!) the gifts were arranged on the table. I expect that was because it was warm downstairs when we were at last allowed to go and see. There was always a huge pork pie for breakfast which we could help ourselves to before Mother came down to start the serious business of Christmas Day. We all went to church and I loved the Christmas carols.

Easter was a serious religious occasion in those days, before it became commercialised. There was the solemn period of Lent to be observed and morning service was a must on Good Friday. By teatime, things lightened a little and we were given traditional hot cross buns for tea made by the local baker. They were only produced and eaten on that day, not all the year round, as now. Then on Palm Sunday, we were given a palm cross at Sunday school and drew pictures of Jesus riding on a donkey. We didn't give gifts or send cards but it was nice to have something new to wear if we were lucky. We always had lamb and green peas and mint sauce for Easter Sunday lunch. It was a day for rejoicing and there was Easter Monday to look forward to.

My main memory is about the shops my parents owned and my Aunt and Uncle kept a general shop under the Horn's Bridge. My sister recalls my parents having a shop on the corner of Warwick Street and Storforth Lane. They sold papers, shoelaces, groceries, sweets and bread. In hard times, people would come in for just half a loaf and ask for credit.

The favourite sweets were sold out of a large sweet jar and wrapped in a square of paper, made into a cone shape and screwed at the bottom. A halfpenny's worth was the amount usually asked for by children as spending money was hard to come by. We would buy boiled sweets and make one last all the way home. Other favourites were sherbet dabs, liquorice laces and sticks, coconut chips and bluebird toffees.

STELLA MOSELEY

I think my earliest memories are of playin round here. I can remember my Grandma Knight sat here where I'm sat now, and I should only be about six when she died. She used to sit here in a wicker chair with her feet on a stool. My Uncle Walter sometimes sent her a box of tangerine oranges and I used to sit on the stool, my mouth watering, I only remember sayin' it once, 'cos I hadn't got to ask, it were bad manners 'I like tangerine oranges Grandma'. 'Do you my love' and she gave me one link. Whether that was for being cheeky I don't know, I had one link. She did have her bed in this room, she died in this
room, in fact somebody's died in every room in this house, so if it's haunted don't blame me (laughs). Yes, I can remember when she died and then there was the funeral, talk about a big funeral, cos it was a big family. A big hearse outside

here with four great big black horses with the plumes, and men on the front with the veils over their faces. All her grandsons, six grandsons carried her into chapel. It must have been warmish weather because I can remember 'em, all the men, you know how men congregate and talk, all in the garden talking. All the women sat cup-a teain' it in here you know 'cos they had big teas in those days, they called 'em wakes you know.

When I was about nine years old I was bridesmaid for my cousin John Bestwick and Harold Knight was his best man. I was on the front of the photos with another little girl called Stella. We had some little pink satin frocks, beautifully embroidered, I think my cousin Hilda made these hats, oh beautiful, with swansdown all round, beautiful they were.

We didn't have many toys, 'cos there weren't a lot of money about. I think we did better than some miner's children because my Dad never went drinkin' you see. I remember seein' drunken men, where their kid's had hardly anythin on their backs. You see wives couldn't go out to work to help in those days. Once a woman found out she was expectin' she couldn't keep her old job, no, she'd got to go. In fact sometimes they wouldn't employ a woman who were married because she might be expectin' and leave 'em in a mess. Nowadays they expect you to work. Well these days you wouldn't be able to buy a house unless a wife was helpin' out, no you wouldn't.

We loved Christmas, me Dad made Christmas. Oh he did, he was like Santa Claus me Dad. We didn't have a lot of presents, me and our Frank and our Dot. Our Irene and our Mave came off best because by the time they were gettin' a bit older, we were growin' up and gettin' a bit of money you see. Our Mave came off best, aye she had allsorts, we saw to that. We hung our stockings up and we had an orange, an apple, and nuts, and new pennies. That were nice, that were a wonderful thing for us, and we'd have p'raps a box of dominoes, or a ludo game, or snakes and ladders. I remember once our Frank had two pigs on string and that were a game (laughs) they were on string with a hook. You hooked it on the end of the table and the string went through these pigs, and you had to keep pulling, and there they were gallopin' across the table. We had some fun with them. Oo, and a bagatelle, he had one of those. I only had one doll in me life, only one doll. yes. I were about five when I had him, he were like a baby doll and I called him Bobby. I think he must have been about eighty when he dropped to pieces (laughs). I found him in the airing cupboard an he were in a sorry state (laughs). Me and our Frank bought our Mavis a Tansad doll's pram, oh beautiful. Babies these days don't have one as good as the doll's pram that our Mave had (laughs) it were a lovely thing. We used to enjoy just bein' all together and a lovely Christmas dinner. You know, a big piece of pork was what we had, and a piece of beef. We didn't get any poultry or anything like that. You know how you can get birds these days, ten a penny practically, a fowl or a goose or anything like that were very rare, they were expensive they were. So we didn't get any of them, but a piece of pork, yeah. I remember, one Christmas we nearly didn' t get the pork. Me Dad went down Town to get this piece of pork and left it on the pavement (laughs). He'd got on the bus and left it on the pavement (laughs). He had to go back and get it, an' it were still there in a brown paper bag, yeah, it were still there (laughs).

We had Easter Eggs at Easter as well. The best we had was down at my Aunt Alice's down Storforth Lane there. We had Easter Egg hunts, oh it were fabulous. We used to go down there and Uncle Will used to hide little nests with eggs in all in different places all over the garden. There we were, we were runnin all over the garden, frantic. We were liftin' the hens out of their nests, lookin' under 'em. He'd put 'em there you know, he'd put 'em anywhere. We'd dive into the big shed 'cos he'd got those great big boxes all for the corn, for his poultry. We'd dive in underneath to get these 'ere eggs. Aunt Alice would sit on the swing in the orchard. She'd sit there with a big white apron on and whenever we found 'em, we couldn't eat them, we'd got to bring 'em to her and drop them in her white overall. She'd be sat there swingin' away, and singin', and there we were, frantically running about searching. Under seats, under cabbages, in the greenhouses, but we did have a good time and then when they'd all been found, we'd share up, fair and square.

We went to Sunday School every Sunday, at the Methodist Chapel when it was in the old buildin'. I used to go there right from when I was three or four. Then as I got older, from Sunday School, the older children went to the mornin' service at Chapel. Uncle Will used to go every Sunday mornin', yeah, and he used to collar me and make me sit at the side of him. Fidgeted and fidgeted, I did, because the seats were hard and me legs didn't reach the floor, they dangled – it were so borin to sit through a sermon. He always used to suck sugared almonds an' I were lucky if I got one, but he used to give me one just to keep me quiet (laughs). Then there were the Anniversaries, recitin', and then from there into the choir. I was in the choir for a long time, yes they was lovely days they were.

I can remember going to school and my Mum takin' me in my pushchair. Yes, and my first school was, you know the old chapel buildings that used to be at the back of The Devonshire, my first school was there. As we went round the corner there was a blacksmith's shop somewhere there. As well there was a house that went down some steps, a very old stone house round that area, because a Mrs Bingham lived there. That school was like a nursery. I think that was about one of the first nurseries maybe, cos I were in the pushchair. I can remember seein' the sparks flying, you know, from the anvil at the blacksmiths, and the clangin' of it, and then we went round to the school. I don't know how long I was there. No I can't remember much about being in there, but I remember when we were moved down to Eyre Street School to go in the proper class down there, I should be about five years old. We were in a crocodile and I can remember walkin' in the crocodile down Kent Street, mm. I can't remember anyone who went to that school at the same time as me. After I'd been down there, then I went up to The Green School. I think they moved you up at about seven years old. Hasland Hall School wasn't a school when I moved to the Junior School. Old Gaffa Bowden, he were headmaster and he lived in that little house at the side, that little stone house that's attached to the school. Oo, he was a strict man he was, but all Hasland children knew how to be polite, they did. He taught them their manners. He taught all Hasland children good manners and he taught 'em how to sing.

I can remember Ascension Day, that was the only time we had a day off anywhere. We used to crocodile down to St. Paul's Church opposite the cemetery. It was a Church of England School you see. Then they made Hasland Hall into a school, and I was one of the first children to go up there into the new school. It was like going into a new world 'cos there was a gym there and like a science room for the boys, and we put proper plays on, you know, in the gym. I was in me glory, oh it were lovely and I loved to be singin' as well, and I was in the school choir. I always remember Gaffer Bowden used to fetch me out of class sometimes 'cos I could hit the high notes then (laughs) I can't now! He used to stand me in a corner and he'd be bangin' notes up on the piano and I was goin higher, and higher, and higher. His idea of standin' you in a corner facin', was your voice hit the walls and it bounced back 'cos it echoed in the gym 'cos it was high. He came up from The Green School with us and I think another teacher came as well. I forget the name of the new headmaster for the Green School 'cos it was like infants and then juniors. You were about twelve when you went up to the Senior School, I think I were about twelve, perhaps a bit more because I don't think I'd been there much above a year when I left. Oh, but it were a lovely year that was. Fair enjoyed that, yeah. I was fourteen when I left school, and I went STRAIGHT TO WORK! (laughs). It were like droppin' from heaven into hell (laughs) crikey, you thought you were hard-worked at school but by jingo!

I started work at Robinsons and I had to go into Robinson's school. I only left school at Christmas and just after the New Year holidays I was straight to work. There were no interval, aye it were Robinson's school up School Board Lane. They had a school to train your abilities, your speed and ability. I had a month there and then arrived into the weavin' sheds, tentin' they called it. I worked there, altogether, apart from my fifteen years, you know havin' my babies, about thirty-four years, praps more, I know a long time. I retired then. Happy days they were, hard working but happy days. They were a good firm, marvellous firm. If you'd any trouble, if you went to them they'd help you. They looked after their employees, definitely, very good. When I went there, there was that Miss Florrie Robinson, she was one of the directors and she were a good lass. She looked after the girls, she did. She ran their drama society, opera, she ran that. She was ever such a good girl she was. When I was working I spent more time at work and up Brampton then, 'cos you spent so many hours at work, You couldn't even get home for your dinner. Sometimes I used to go, when it were Summertime, to the baths up there. I used to go and have a bit of a swim up there for an hour and then have my lunch when I got back.

We used to go to a dance now and then, 'cos me Mam didn't like these little hops. She'd let me go to a nice dance. They used to have some nice dances at the Victoria Ballroom, half a crown do's, evening dress they were, yes, they were lovely, lovely dance floor as well and Stan Cox's Band. Sometimes towards Christmas time there'd be a dinner dance and they were nice, evening dress. There were these little dances as well that I went to now and then. There was one above Boden's chip shop, on the corner there, that was nice. I liked that and me Mam did let me go there sometimes because it was more of a religious meetin' there, and funds went for that community there. There were two great big fires in that room, it was cosy but we did have some fun there. There was Bradbury Hall, I went once or twice there but it was a bit too far to walk, and you were hangin' about waitin' for buses ages so I didn't bother much. We went to the pictures in Hasland, and the Odeon in Town. There was the Odeon where the Winding Wheel is now, and the Regal where the Zanzibar is now. They're all weird names to me now, yeah. Then there was the Corporation Theatre, where the theatre is now, Pomegranate, yeah we used to go there but not a lot because by then me Mum were very poorly.

I was twenty-one when me Mam died but I was only seventeen when she had her strokes you know, and it was terrible. I always felt sorry for me Mam because, I mean, she'd got a young family and couldn't do for 'em. It must have been absolutely frustrating and horrible. She were only forty-seven when she died. Me Dad and our Frank were on shift work at the pit you see, at Grassmoor. Me Dad did have some time at Holmewood but he finished at Grassmoor. Our Frank moved to Markham Area Workshops. I can remember him sayin' just before he died, he wanted to flog his bike because it was hard work gettin' there, it were uphill and it were gettin' a bit too much for him. He were only forty-five when he died so he wasn't well himself.

There was a Feast held on the front of The Devonshire, and then against the Central Garages before they built those corporation houses, and then outside the New Inn, at the back of the New Inn. Also before Mr Smith took over the Club fields at the end of Smithfield Avenue, they had this big ground for the feast. I know boys used to jump over the school wall to get in because they used to get free rides sometimes, they used to help the men there. The big whales came there, I've never seen a whale since then, great big things trundlin round. Yes, great big whales with seats in and you just went up and down. There were flying chairs, then there were the cranky horses and there was a giant's stride. There was the helter skelter, I loved that helter skelter, I spent all my pennies on that. There were side shows, brandy snaps, hot peas, coconut stalls, there were everythin' there. My Dad, he could knock a coconut off, and I think he knocked coconuts off for all the street, but yes that was a lovely Feast. Then of course it stopped, and there were no Feast for a while. The field belonged to Hasland Club and there was a big gate. That was before all Smithfield Avenue were built. It was a wonderful thing that was. Everything seemed to stop when War broke out, everythin', because of the lights, and everythin was blacked out. The War changed our lives a lot. Everythin' started coming to a different turnin'. Everythin' started to sort of drop off, no food, no buses into Town, no petrol and things like that. More hours, workin more hours. I mean, I don't remember much only work, twelve hours, twelve hour shifts. I was in the weaving sheds and they wanted all bandages, lint, field dressings, everythin'. Of course my husband Jack was down at Brian Donkins at first, then he was drafted to Derby and he was there till forty-five.

We got married in forty-two and that were a toss-up whether we could get married or not because there were no food about and everythin' were coupons. Clothes were coupons, but everybody were ever so good, they all seemed to scrat up and got me the coupons for a nice bridal dress and bridesmaid dresses. Then everybody was ever so good with fruit and stuff, an egg here, and an egg there, to make a wedding cake. Mrs Cox off Eyre Street, she made my cake and, oh aye, everybody were ever so good. We didn't go away afterwards, ee no, 'was your journey really necessary', you couldn't go anywhere, no, you couldn't travel. You had to have permits if you wanted to go anywhere. When we were first married there was no room here with my Dad so we went and stopped with Jack's Mum and Dad down Calow Lane. My sister Mavis cried her eyes out, she thought when I got married she weren't going to see me any more (laughs). Yes it was hard going, first off during the War till we got sort of used to it. I can remember my Dad went up Kent Street instead of our street, in the black-out, and walked into somebody's house for his supper (laughs). You used to have to have little badges, fluorescent, sort of shone up in the dark, and if you had a little flash lamp you'd got to put a piece of paper round the glass so that there was just a little bit of light no thicker than a pencil shone through. Every house was blacked out, you had to put black-outs up to your windows. My Dad made a frame and put some like brattice cloth to fix up to the window outside, and he'd peg it in with a little peg each side. Of course you couldn't do upstairs, we had to have really thick curtains for upstairs. Then we had the air raid wardens comin' round 'PUT THAT LIGHT OUT'. I did know that Harry Heath who lived across here, he were a warden for this area. One night I didn't realise it was gettin' as dark as what it was, and I'd gone upstairs and put the bedroom light on. I had the back bedroom here, and I thought 'Oo, it's dark, the blackout', drew one curtain and this voice said 'PUT THAT LIGHT OUT, I'LL HAVE YOU UP'. It was Harry. I said 'What the hell do you think I'm doing? SHEW!' and I pulled the curtains across. Oo, he did make me mad, the fathead, what did he think I were up at the window for, the chump! Anyway, we had some laughs.

Jack could remember when Coppings had got like a little kiosk across the road. Yeah, he could remember that. I can't remember that, I can only remember Coppings being where it is now but it was only small, they sort of extended over time. Next to Coppings you went up those stairs to a billiard hall, it were a billiard hall there then, where men used to go and play billiards. Joe Davis played up there. My Jack used to go up there when he were younger, when he d left school he liked to play billiards.

When it were Christmas time and me and our Dot were old enough we'd go round Chistmas singin'. I don't think we were bad little singers and we give 'em one or two Christmas hymns so we'd get quite a few pennies. We used to take our money and go to Miss Copes and in there she used to have chocolate Santa Claus, about a ha'penny or a penny each, for Christmastime, and spice pigs. Me and our Dot would have our noses pressed to that window looking at these chocolate Santa Claus, and we'd go and get one. In Copes they had all like pastries that were fresh, fresh pastries, vanillas and cream slices, oo! We couldn't afford 'em, we tried not to look at them 'cos we couldn't afford 'em. Mr Chambers on the front, went to the shop next to Coppings, 'cos he had a bike shop on the front, first off, yes, just past the Co-op. Where the Pet Shop is now, was Redfern's butchers, that's another thing, we had about seven butcher's shops in Hasland, we haven't got one now. Not one, and on every corner there was a butcher's shop, even two in our street. There were Gothards at the bottom of York Street and then Frank Fearn at the top. Then there was Shentalls on the front, and then there was Laits shop that sold papers and cigarettes and things. Then Needhams, 'cos we used to get some nice little dresses from there, and overalls. There were allsorts, and it were a good size, a biggish shop. Then where that bay window is, there were two bays at one time, one at the bottom and one at the top, that was Harold's shoe shop and they had some lovely shoes in there. Next was Wilbourne's chemist shop. Right at the end where Marco's is now, there were McKays and they had all ladies underwear, corsets, boned corsets oo! The other side of the shop was men's clothes, overalls, caps, underwear, allsorts. The Co-op was across the road where it is now but they also sold clothes in the part next door, they had shoes, overalls, coats and hats. At that time most of the people who owned the shops lived above. You'd no need to go down Town for anythin', Hasland were self-sufficient with food and everythin'. It was a lovely village, it still is except we haven't got a butcher's shop.

We used to have a band every Sunday in the bandstand in Hasland Park, and the Park was certainly used in those days. There was the Baptists, there was our Chapel, even the Church an' they always used to come out on a Sunday night and all make for the park and walk round, because it was a round path then. There were railings all round the bandstand, and little deckchairs if you wanted to go and sit and listen. It got full, yeah, we used to go and listen 'cos Hasland Silver Prize Band was a wonderful band, we were always proud of that band, I can remember that. Then there was Al Needham, an' he lived just up the street 'ere with his mother, and we could hear him practicin' on his trumpet, yeah. Oh there was a lot of music in them days, they was lovely days.

Hasland were a lovely place to grow up in, everybody knew one another. It's always been friendly and everybody knew one another. Oo, I m glad I didn't go any-where else, it has been a lovely place. I knew everybody and as I say you'd no need to go anywhere for anythin', it was all 'ere. I mean they used to have dances down at the Village Hall, you weren't forced to go out of the village. There was Hasland pictures, there were about two or three pictures a week, changed over so you'd plenty of entertainment. In the Summertime there was the tennis, tennis club and tennis courts. There was one in the park and there was one over that stone stile, in Parker's field on Hasland Green. There was quite enough to do. Of course, as well, the Grassmoor lads used to come down to Hasland after the girls and the Hasland boys used to go up Grassmoor after the girls, a little bit of a swop-over, so it were quite nice (laughs).

ROBERT WOOD

Can you tell me what your earliest memory is?

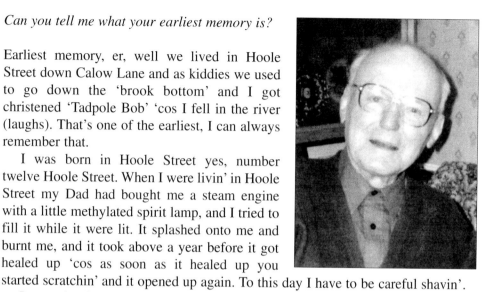

Earliest memory, er, well we lived in Hoole Street down Calow Lane and as kiddies we used to go down the 'brook bottom' and I got christened 'Tadpole Bob' 'cos I fell in the river (laughs). That's one of the earliest, I can always remember that.

I was born in Hoole Street yes, number twelve Hoole Street. When I were livin' in Hoole Street my Dad had bought me a steam engine with a little methylated spirit lamp, and I tried to fill it while it were lit. It splashed onto me and burnt me, and it took above a year before it got healed up 'cos as soon as it healed up you started scratchin' and it opened up again. To this day I have to be careful shavin'.

I started school at the back of The Devonshire, the Methodist Chapel, that's where I started school. It was religious as well. There was seatin' right the way round it if you remember, well at break time you had to lie down on the seats and go to sleep for ten minutes. When my mother took me on the first day I beat my Mother home, I were back home before she were (laughs). Then we went to Eyre Street of course. While we were there, our nature walk was down Hasland Green, and you know that little walk on the back that comes back onto Storforth Lane, well that was our nature walk back up the fields. We'd occasionally come in the Park, but not very often. Then from Eyre Street I went up to The Green School, the Hall School wasn't there then. They were just startin' The Hall when I finished. I left school when I were fourteen. Mr Bowden, the headmaster of the Green School was a singin' fanatic. At singin lessons he'd walk into the class, or whatever class it were, and he'd stand at the back of you, and at every singing lesson you were supposed to go out the front. Mr Cooper were our teacher, and it were a singin' lesson this particular day. Mr Bowden come walkin' out, his office were inside our class at the time. I ran to the front an' I were in my place, singin' away. He come to me and said 'Righto Wood come on down, hold your hand out. You'll learn one of these days.' Four strokes (laughs). Lord Bowden that was his son, oh he did very, very well for himself, and he had a daughter. He was regimentated you know, oh and he ruined the lass's life, she walked so stiff. She got to be headmistress at Brimington Common School.

The biggest part of our kiddies life was spent down Calow Lane on the brook bottom, I knew every blade of grass on there, owd Sally Walker's Farm, Gorse Farm. Instead of goin up the path we'd go along the brook bottom and she could see us down in the bottom and she'd say 'Fetch the gun Reg I'll shoot the buggers'. (laughs) I was a notorious character you know. We got summonsed by that Mrs Walker down Calow Lane. There were six of us and we were down Calow Lane, we were gettin' timber for the bonfire. There was a log in the river just over the bridge so we went down to the river and fetched this log out. Mrs Walker spotted us. Anyway on Sunday mornin' the police come to our house with summonses. We had to go to Brimington Road Police Station and we didn't know where it were, anyway we found it. Me Mother went with us. Nowadays they wouldn't have got away with it. Anyway it finished up, they decided to fine us twelve shillin', six shillin' damages and six shillin' costs. Well that were a lot of money then. Anyway my mother paid mine and that settled that. About six months after we were just havin' us dinner in Hoole Street, a knock come to the door, it were little Ernest Wright. 'Can tha come with me Bob'. 'Why' I said. 'We've got to go and fetch me dad out of jail'. His dad hadn't paid the fine you see. We went on the fields right through to Brimington, Infirmary Road. Anyway, when we got there it were about quart' to five 'You don't want to be here you want to be at Beetwell Street' they said. We didn't know you see, we never went to Town then you know. Anyway, we finally got there at five minutes to five and Mr Wright played holy diddle. 'Who's told you, who's paid?' He played hell, aye. So ever since that, I always say I've been to jail (laughs).

I loved Christmas, oh aye, all the family loved Christmas of course, I'd three brothers and two sisters. We didn' t have a deal though, there were very, very little. Some coppers in the bottom of a stockin, that were about it. My Mother was born on Hipper Street in Chesterfield, you know the bus depot, Britannia Buildings, there was a big house at the end. There were two rows of old cottages backed onto what is now the bus stand, and this big house at the end. That were my Grandma's, and my Grandad, he was commissionaire at the Corporation Theatre. Yes he was the commissionaire at the Civic. When we used to go, when it went onto films it were always westerns, always westerns there. The theatre was round, as you know there were boxes at each side. It were marvellous like. We used to go to my Grandma's of course down at Beetwell Street occasionally. She lived on her own when I can remember her, she lived to be a big age. I never actually knew a Grandad. I knew both Grandma's, the other one lived at Heaton Street at Brampton. But we didn't visit Grandparents very often, they were too far away you see and you couldn't afford a bus there, penny bus fare, oh no. We'd walk it to Town occasionally. My Mother used to go Sat'dy shoppin', yes and I used to have to meet her off the bus with the shoppin' bag, aye.

We didn't have any holidays when I were little. I tell you the first place we went to, I have vivid memories of that it was with St. Paul's Church in Hasland, the first trip out of Hasland. We had about sixteen buses and every body went on it. Whitworth Institute, Darley Dale we went to. It were a big outin' that were, yes. There were sixteen 'yella belly' buses, East Midland buses. It weren't East Midland it were a private firm then. Aye, we had a right good time, it were marvellous. Oh, the year I went in the Army I went to Blackpool. We'd been workin' on Unstone viaduct for about sixteen or eighteen weeks. When it were done my Mother said 'You want to get off on holiday, you've earnt some money'. Well, the lads, down Calow Lane, they arranged to go as well, but gradually one dropped out, two dropped out, you know. Finished up there were only me. Well my Mother said 'I'll write to Mrs Drabble'. That were where my Mother and Father used to go, to Lord Street in Blackpool. At any rate, she wrote to her and I got in. It were the best holiday I had in my life, I went on my own. I met two lads from Wigan and until a few years ago I were still getting a card at Christmas from them. The second night we were there, we were in the Tower Ballroom, upstairs there. I couldn't dance you see, and Les said 'Come on Bob' and we got up and danced together (laughs) and they chucked us out. Two men dancing together (laughs). But we had a marvellous holiday, it were brilliant.

When I left school, I'd be fourteen then, my first few weeks I had on the belts at Grassmoor, course it were only a week or two and then they stood you off for the Summer. Anyway when I were about fifteen, we were playin' in the street and my Mother come and shouted me. She said 'Get off up to Hasland to see Mr Cope there's a job for you'. So I went. He used to have that little shop at the bottom of the Billiard Hall steps, and he put his daughter in that little shop. He'd two daughters. Anyway when I went to see Mr Cope he said 'I were wonderin' when tha were gunna come' he said 'Somebody told me tha wanted a job, I wondered when tha were gunna come'. Any way, I started, eight shillings a week at Woodheads. It were all walk, and Billy Thomas, he worked at the Co-op, he started at The Co-op and I started at Woodheads. We still laugh about it when I see him, I say 'He were a rich man, Billy were, he had a bike and I had a barrow' (laughs). That's how I got to know Mary Hallam, she lived at the farm at the bottom of Raise Hill, goin' towards Calow, Wildgoose the farmer's name were. She used to come round to Woodheads in the car, every week, and order two stone of flour. They'd say 'Yes Robert'll bring it, two stone of flour.' Anyway, I used to take it on the barrow to the bottom of the hill, get one stone out and carry it up the hill. I were just about leavin' when they provided a bike. Any way, I used to put my barrow in Charlie Hallam's yard and that's how I got to know 'em you see. Then, it were years after, in fact I'd come out of the Army and I had to go down there, I took a bit of scrap in. Anyway, the old lady, Polly, Charlie Hallam's wife, she used to smoke a clay pipe. She were sortin' this scrap out and she'd got an axle, a car axle. She said 'Give me a lift up with this Bob' I said 'What you doin'.' She said 'Chuckin' it in the bin'. I said 'No you want to take that to pieces'. She said 'Why' so I said 'Well, the crown wheel and pinion in that are phosphorous bronze'. She thought it were all in scrap steel you see. She said 'A tha all rait, a tha sure?' (laughs) I said 'I'm certain Mrs Hallam'. 'Right' she says. I were her pal for life after that. It were worth about twenty quid that were, even then.

We traded with Shentall's shop, that which is now One-Stop. Chesterfield was the main depot for Shentalls and they had their own bakery at the back of the shop in Chesterfield and their pork pies were very, very good. They never give any divi or anythin' like that. Then Shentalls become JSL. They started givin' gifts away with coupons, that were the first thing. A lot of people went there then. Mr Cope were still the manager at Woodheads, his two daughters worked in his little shop. One, Vivienne she were a beautiful girl and she had a very poor childhood, you know, she was an invalid, but she made a good job of the shop, aye. Then there was Doris, we used to call her Dori. Vivienne was a bit older than Doris, aye. There were three daughters the other one, she were taller than them two and she married Cliff Scothern. I used to play the organ at St. Paul's Church then you know, and Cliff Scothern got the organist's job there. 'Let em all go, Bob' he'd say, and then he'd start talkin' about Reg Dixon and he used to dance (laughs). He couldn't half play it, aye, he could. We were big pals me and old Cliff. His parents had the shop at Grassmoor, right facing Birkin Lane. That corner shop agen the Picture Palace, that were their shop, yes, that's where he come from.

There were lots of butcher's shops in Hasland then. Yes, there were one, two, three, four butcher's shops. The first one goin' from the Toll Bar is the first shop on the right-hand side, that was Norman's. He used to sell foreign meat, it used to come in squares, it was solid, but it made a beautiful meat and tata pie (laughs). You'd get a shillin's worth. Then course there were John Shentalls, then there were Coppings, and then the Billiard Hall and then Copes. Then onto The Green there were Darnell's greengrocers and of course the Post Office on the end. Mr Smith's barber's shop was in between them. He was an agent for the Railway you know, and you'd be halfway through your haircut when somebody would come and want a ticket (laughs). Anyway then, across the road, what is now the trophy shop, that was a panshion shop, earthenware, peggy pots and panshions and all that. Then you come onto the corner shop, that was a butcher's shop, Redferns, and a one-armed, one-eyed chap used to keep it. He'd a patch over his eye. Then you went round the corner to Woodheads, next was the paper shop. Beetons were the last most popular one there, but the one before that was Nuttalls. Billy Nuttall. Further up there was a millinery shop, and then you went on to the chemist, Wilbournes, Mr Wilbourne. Next door was McKays, Mr McKay was off Hasland Green and he had two daughters. I could take you right to their house, aye. Then all them other shops have come over the years you see. I remember the cobblers, as well. Then of course there was a monumentalist always lived at the top of Calow Lane. Then across from that there was Lowes butchers shop. Then Normans again, at the bottom of Chapel Lane. On Hampton Street, where the carpet shop is, that was Mr Fearn's butcher s shop there. Gothard's butcher s shop was down at the bottom of York Street. They all killed on site. We used to sit on the wall and watch 'em kill the cows when we were kids, aye. Course they used to buy some old bulls and all that, and they used to have a ring in the floor and they used to fasten the rope onto it's nose and pull it's head down to the floor you see while they killed it. It were a right performance.

We left Hoole Street when I was about sixteen and we went to Wingerworth.

Then I were workin', errand-laddin' at Woodheads at the Toll Bar. I walked from there to Wingerworth at least four times a day across them fields day and night. Then when I got to seventeen, eighteen I liked the job but there were no money only about eight shillin' a week. So anyway a job come vacant with the plumber at the railway and I got it. I started up there about eighteen years old with the old plumber. When I worked on the railway we were based at Chesterfield. Then when I come out of the Army there wasn't a vacancy at Chesterfield, there were one at Ambergate, so I went to Ambergate for four year. Then one mornin my gaffer at Ambergate Jimmy Hunt, we were big pals, he said 'I've got a letter here Bob your stations Chesterfield from next week.' He were really mad he were. He said 'I just get ones I like to work with and then they take 'em off me.' They sent me back to Chesterfield and then eventually Sheffield took us all over, but we stopped at Chesterfield, it was like a sub-station.

Then when the War came they had me back that winter 'cos it was a bad winter 1939-40. I was a reserve and I volunteered to go in the Railway Operatin' Department. I had a medical for it and then they sent me a letter, 'Owin' to the adverse weather conditions you're goin' to be retained until further notice.' Well I didn't go up while August, I went and joined the Lincoln Regiment. Then they'd come out and ask you for tradesmen, to move onto a trade so of course I went out. They said 'All we've got in your line is coppersmiths, would you like to go on a course for coppersmiths?' So I went on a coppersmith's course to Glasgow, and he was a grand old chap actually who was in charge. He'd got a system as he had teachin', it were brilliant. There were twelve vices round this shed or this workshop, and you got to this vice. He'd put whatever you'd got to work on that day, and you cleaned it up, stripped it down or whatever, then you'd move to the next vice. Then you'd got to put it together again, somebody else's you see. We always used to eat a packet of sandwiches in the middle of the day, same thing every day. He said 'I don't have that lads I have puddin'. Puddin', every day. When you're poorly, what do you they give you? Puddin' I can hear him now (laughs). Anyway I passed that and they found out they'd got too many coppersmiths, so would we mind going on an NV fitter's course. So I said 'Aye, I'll go to school, I'm not faitin' while I'm going to school.' (laughs). So I went to Glasgow again Sauchiehall Street. I was in civvy billets at the back of Rangers Football ground. Mrs McCulluch, Ibrox Oval. I were there three months, and they went to school on Sauchiehall Street, Stowe Colleges. I passed that, then I had the final three months at Manchester an' I were in civvy billets on Moss Side there. Because I worked on the railway I got PT's. I could come home every weekend when I wasn't on duty. I could come home Sat'dy till Monday mornin'. So long as I were back for Monday mornin' I were alright. So that were that. Then next thing he says 'Right, he's had a good time this lad, Northern Ireland next stop.' (laughs). But it wasn't too bad, and then we come back and we started preparin' tanks for the invasion, we waterproofed 'em. We went right up in the North of Scotland and it was terrible, it was a dry cold but we never took no harm, you know. We were sleeping in Nissan huts and icicles were hanging down, oh dear. Your clothes, your bed steamed, you know (laughs) oh it were terrible.

Then we went. It were 27th Armoured Brigade. When we'd finished all the tanks, done 'em all, they were all loaded up. We loaded 'em onto a train and we brought 'em down to Petworth in Surrey. We were there finishin' off, tidying up for about a couple of months. Then we took 'em down to the coast and loaded em on the boats, bobbin' up and down for about a month. Then we went for the invasion. We landed on D6, just outside Plumetot, Aramanchus Beach, and we stopped there for about ten days. Then we went straight into Brussels. Our HQ was Brussels for eight or nine months, never moved. We were goin' out servicin' tanks, you see, repairin' 'em on the job. There were some rough times but we had some good times as well, yes. We got some nice friends in Brussels. Madame and Monsieur Houdart they were, just outside Wemmel, Brussels. We got the tanks all ready for crossin the Rhine. We had to test 'em in the water at the King of Brussel's palace, in his lake, but we got one fast, stuck rait in the middle of the lake. Old Billy Rhodes, our captain, he was a beautiful chap, an' it were cold, very cold and he said 'Well there's only one thing lads somebody looks like gettin' their clothes off'. It were breakin' all the ropes and chains, tryin to pull it out. Anyway he stripped off, and he were whiter than that ceiling (laughs). But he went in and I went in with him, and do you know what it was? It were a shingle bottom and the pebbles had rolled into the track, and the rollers wouldn't go over them, you see.

I come home on leave from there to get married. Then, well I wasn't back six months before I got demobbed and there was our Jean, she were born in Scarsdale Maternity Home. Evelyn come out of the Maternity Home into this house, straight into this house. We got chance of this house. It belonged to Dorothy Lowe from Elm Tree Farm, she were a teacher at Tapton House School. I'd noticed this cottage, there were a tree growing out of that door, it were really down, you know. What had happened, Dorothy Lowe's brother bought it at an auction at The Devonshire for £500. When he died he left it in his will to Dorothy, but it had been empty for quite a while and had become derelict. Anyway it must have been in 1957 and I should have been at work that Sunday morning. I never went, I went to see Dorothy. 'Now then Mr Wood I understand that you're interested in the cottage, well I'd like somebody to look after it and I know you will'. She said 'My brother bought it for £500 how will 550 do you'. We shook hands on it there and then and she gave me the deeds and the lot. She said 'Take them to Mr Bradley tomorrow'.

It were very, very nice growin up in Hasland, yes it were very, very good. Same as I say, Hoole Street it had it's own group of neighbours they were as good as gold, neighbourly. There were Mrs Clay she nursed everybody in Hoole Street and she put 'em away, you know. That's how it was then, yes. Anybody sick, Mrs Clay. You couldn't afford a doctor, no. They came to my Mother as well, they used to rattle on the door. I'll never forget it, Betty Hall lived next door. Had a farm at the bottom of Calow Lane. They had a daughter Betty, she died about three year old. My Mum sat up with her for, oh, two or three weeks aye. There were some right characters in Hoole Street, they'd set to in the middle of the street and then they'd be goin out together (laughs).